To my kids, James, Leland, and Azalea,

and my husband, Michael. You're

my reason why and my

compass when I

need one.

Contents

CHAPTER SIX

Operation Permission to Pause

CHAPTER SEVEN

Staying on Target

CHAPTER ONE

Are You Ready to Become a Bounceback Parent?

WELCOME, RECRUIT!

Are you ready to feel more capable and confident, and less overwhelmed and guilty as a parent? Are you ready for connection, not perfection? You're in the right place!

You hold in your hands a field guide that will help you become a Bounceback Parent who can embrace a mindset of growth and learning. Bounceback Parents are all about connection, not perfection. This way of thinking about parenting tends to help people lighten up and enjoy parenting more.

Hi, I'm Alissa Marquess, a mom to three and the founder of Bounceback Parenting. I'm so glad you've joined us. I'll serve as your director of ops for Bounceback Parenting League.

Why Bounceback Parenting?

When I first had kids, I was totally unprepared for the huge emotional upheaval I was thrown into. I found myself struggling to learn how to deal with anger and fears I'd never experienced (at least not at this level) and learning how to take care of myself while caring for small people, all while frequently being utterly exhausted. Oh, and I wanted to be a connected, loving mom too.

What I didn't know at the beginning of this journey is that parenting would be the ultimate training in resilience. I had to learn to bounce back over and over again when I would stumble, and I've stumbled a lot.

Sometimes bouncing back has been extremely humbling; I've had to reexamine my assumptions and change my perspective. Sometimes it's been invigorating when I can bounce back with more knowledge, a new parenting tool, or a deeper commitment to building the connected relationships I treasure. Either way I'm always learning, and to me, being a Bounceback Parent means seeing the challenges in parenting as opportunities for growth. I believe everybody is capable of growing and learning, starting from right where they are.

All of the missions in this book will lead you to a Bounceback Parenting outlook. The Bounceback Parenting framework gives you the ability to be a work in progress yet also enjoy your kids and parenting as you learn.

Bounceback Parenting Credo

We build resilient, connected families by having a growth mindset in parenting.

- **We believe everyone can learn and grow, starting from right where they are**—by choosing to look at past mistakes and current challenges not as indications of failure but as the foundation for growth and resilience.
- **We seek out everyday connections**—by finding joy in the ordinary, nurturing open communication, and looking for unexpected moments to connect.
- **We practice compassionate self-care**—by getting to know and accept ourselves, learning to notice our own needs, and taking steps to tend to those needs.
- **We empower others**—by building on strengths, allowing for growth, and expecting the best from the people around us.
- **We give ourselves permission to pause**—by reflecting on what we've learned, celebrating wins and honoring losses, and creating space to be intentional.

Connection, not perfection!

Why *Secret Missions*?

As a mom, I sometimes take myself way too seriously. Parenting is the task I was determined to do perfectly. So when I had kids, I buckled down to be a good mom.

Only problem was . . . what the heck did that mean?

I looked outward, grasping at one style of parenting or another, trying to match myself to their standards. I craved so badly some assurance that I was more than just okay; I wanted to know I was a really good mom.

And any time I would make a mistake it felt horrible.

I felt guilty that I wasn't living up to my own expectations, much less those of the people around me.

Finally, I cracked.

The picture I had built up in my mind of a good mom was so huge that it crushed me. And, thankfully, that's what changed my mindset.

I had to make a change in order to stop feeling resentful and exhausted. I started to look for small, everyday actions I could take to improve and stopped trying to constantly measure up to such huge ideals.

The idea of parenting secret missions was part of my arsenal for changing my mindset. Sometimes we need to surprise ourselves out of a perfection mindset.

Rather than feeling like I had to be perfect and revamp everything I was doing, I'd come up with a secret mission for myself to let me lighten up and experiment a little bit.

Over time my mindset changed, and this has been key to becoming a Bounceback Parent. Instead of looking at our mistakes or missteps as indication that our parenting is doomed, we need a growth mindset about parenting. Parenting secret missions let you take this on.

When you do a mission in this book, think like you're an investigating agent making observations and staying curious. You can ask, "What will this do? How will it work for me?" Give something a try; see how you feel and jot notes in your field guide about your experience. The missions are low-risk, with the potential of high rewards, and most important, they get you unstuck.

How to Use This Field Guide

All the operations, briefings, and missions in this book will lead you toward connection, not perfection. You can read it in order, or pick it up to "bounce back" when your parenting is feeling heavy or off track.

Connection, not perfection.

Consider starting with basic training to learn about the growth mindset, as this will be a theme throughout the book, but if you are feeling a particular need for any section, jump right into it.

You'll find symbols throughout the book for easy navigation.

Indicates a secret mission. You'll be able to see from the title what the objective of the mission is. When you see one of these symbols, put on your investigative-agent thinking cap: get curious and get ready to shift perspective on something in parenting.

✔️ Each mission contains one or two assignments. When you see this symbol, you'll know this is a specific way to take action.

🖊️ Each operation contains field notes sections with journal prompts as well. You can write on these pages, add inspirational quotes, and answer the questions to make this book your own. This will help you apply operation insights to your unique family and situations.

🚩 When you see this symbol, it indicates that you can find more resources in our online headquarters at bouncebackparenting.com /HQ.

Permission Slip

I want this book to be a notebook for you—a book used, reused, dog-eared, and tattered, and then flipped through again. Pages scribbled all over on the front and the back and notes taken. I give you permission right now to write in this book and bookmark your favorite pages. I give you permission to open it in the middle or read it from back to front.

One more tip: The most powerful tool I've found for continually growing my ability to parent positively is to do a weekly check-in. You can find a format for doing your own weekly check-in in chapter five, "Operation Pumpkin Seed." As you work through this book, I suggest taking up the habit of checking in with yourself each week. Grab a notebook so you can keep these reflections together. This can be simple and take a short amount of time. Each week look back and look forward. In this way you'll be able to be more patient with yourself as you see that you are making progress. You can find printable weekly check-in pages at the online head-quarters.

Remember to have fun. The idea of this book and its missions is to remind you that parenting involves trial and error. Try something new in a secret mission and smile, because no one will know what you're up to.

So let's get started. The only way you can learn is by taking action. You don't have to be perfect. Each time you try one of the missions or write down observations in a field notes section you'll improve your Bounceback Parenting skills, leading to closer and more con-nected relationships with your kids.

CHAPTER TWO

Basic Training:
Parenting with a Growth Mindset

MESSAGE FROM OPS
Welcome to basic training. Here we'll tackle the most important part of your Bounceback Parenting education.

- You'll be trained on the growth mindset in parenting and find out how its opposite, the fixed mindset, makes everything harder.
- You'll learn to recognize the villainous Should Mama, who is determined to make parents' lives miserable by reminding them of all the things they should be doing.
- And you'll find out how having a growth mindset makes decision making easier, allowing you to see opportunities for growth instead of becoming paralyzed.

Parenting is one area we all long to get right. Even if we're open to trial and error in other parts of our lives, we'd like to parent perfectly. And so we read and question and strive, adding one *should* after another to our "be a good parent" list.

Soon, not only do we know what we should be doing, we can see all the ways we're not doing it. Or we're doing it wrong. Or we're discovering that what "should" work according to others doesn't work for our family.

Then the guilt descends. In this swirl of guilt and self-doubt, we can no longer see a way forward. We lose trust in ourselves to make choices for our family and get stuck going in circles on a path clouded by guilt. It is the path away from growth.

This is why we need to banish the *shoulds*, let go of how we thought parenting would be, and look toward possibilities for learning. That's what we'll begin in this section—we'll take on a growth mindset, to find our way free of the guilt-and-judgment path and start down one that offers possibility and growth.

What's a Growth Mindset?

The growth mindset is the underlying theme to all our parenting secret missions. In short—a growth mindset means everyone can learn and grow, starting from right where they are.

According to psychologist Dr. Carol Dweck, we can adopt either a fixed or a growth mindset.

People with a fixed mindset believe intelligence and abilities are set, and spend their time trying to prove they have those traits—instead of working to improve them.

People with a growth mindset believe intelligence and abilities can be improved through effort and hard work. This mindset lets people develop resilience and a love of learning.

The neat thing is, just by knowing about the growth mindset, we can move toward having one. We don't have to know everything, because everyone is capable of growing and learning. We can try new things, let go of things if they don't work for us, laugh a little, and try again.

One of my frustrations when I started learning to parent more positively with my kids was the feeling of reading a positive parenting idea and thinking, *Yeah, that would be great if I had the patience of a saint.*

Or being in a situation where I was so angry, and knowing there was probably a better way to handle the situation with my kids, but having no idea what that way might be. I'd feel even more angry, guilty, and discouraged as I worried that I was handling it all wrong.

What I was missing at the time was a growth mindset. I was stuck in a fixed mindset and believed there was a right way to parent, and when I made a mistake it meant I was failing. I didn't yet have the habit of saying to myself: *I will keep learning, and we'll get better at this.*

As I began to see that indeed I did improve in being able to handle anger, tantrums, communication, and more, I developed a growth mindset and began trusting myself—I *could* keep learning. You can trust yourself too—you will keep learning and improving.

FIXED MINDSET PARENTING EXAMPLES

See if you identify with any of these beliefs indicating a *fixed mindset*—but don't worry if you do; you can change your mindset!

- You are inherently a good parent or a bad parent. You try to prove to the world that you *are* a good parent, because if you make mistakes it indicates that maybe you just aren't cut out for this job.

- Connection with your family should happen automatically. If you need to work at your relationships, it means you are failing.
- You are doomed to repeat mistakes that adults made in your life when you were a child.
- Personalities are fixed. For instance, "I have a bad temper, so my kids will have bad tempers."

GROWTH MINDSET PARENTING EXAMPLES

These are the antidotes to having a fixed mindset about parenting!

- Good parenting is not a set gift that some people have and others lack. Parenting skills can be learned.

  Parenting skills can be learned.

- Relationship and communication skills can be learned and improved.
- The problems and issues that arise in families bring opportunities to learn and grow.
- We can trust in the potential of parents and children to grow toward their best selves.

Mission: Grow Your Growth Mindset

To develop a growth mindset in parenting, it's helpful to have a collection of phrases that remind you you're always capable of learning and growth.

Here are some things you can say to yourself.

- I'm in tune with my children, and I'm always looking for the adjustments we can make to improve our family life.
- I made a mistake, and I'm a big enough person to learn from it and move forward instead of clinging to something that isn't working.
- This used to work for us, or I thought this would work for us, but now it doesn't. I can make a change when things aren't working.

Every time you make a mistake, every time you fall flat on your parenting face, you are opening the door to a new opportunity to learn. What a great example of lifelong learning! Isn't that what we want our children to see—how to continue learning and growing all through their lives?

MORE PHRASES THAT ENCOURAGE GROWTH

- I am a work in progress, and this is part of that progress.
- Always learning!
- We can all improve with effort.
- I always have potential for growth.
- What have I learned from this?
- Mistakes mean I'm learning.
- Fail fast and learn quickly.
- I'm showing my kids how to keep learning.
- We're learning together.
- We are a family of learners, and we value mistakes.

✔ Your Assignment:
Choose a Growth Mindset Phrase

Choose a phrase that reminds you of the growth mindset. Write your favorite phrase on a note, take a picture of it, and make it your phone home screen. When you find yourself getting upset about mistakes or uncertainty, refer back to your growth mindset phrase and use it to change your thinking.

Letting Go of How I Thought It Would Be

I started out parenting with stars in my eyes. I believed if I just tried hard enough, I could do everything right and not make any mistakes. In fact, I built it up as the one thing I could not make mistakes in. I'd do it right! And everything would be cozy! And nice! And . . . perfect! I would be the envy of my other parent friends because I would do it "right."

And then I had my first baby.

And oh man, everything was emotions and sleeplessness. It immediately became apparent that having a kid was not going to be just how I thought it would be. I felt jumbled and fearful; I was pretty sure I was doing it wrong, certainly not perfectly. I longed to feel competent again instead of confused.

Survival Mode

Years passed filled with ups and downs, sweetness and spit-up, and adding two more kids to our family.

I kept looking for the perfect solution to things like sleep, tantrums, eating . . . Each time I thought I had it figured out though, things would change, my kids would hit a new stage, and I'd be back to searching for another solution.

One day, I realized I was spending most of my time in survival mode, not enjoying the moment, enduring my kids rather than noticing them, and anxious the whole time that I was screwing it all up. I was worried I'd be filled with regret later if I couldn't stop feeling so frantic and exhausted.

I needed a starting place to change how I was feeling. I didn't want to spend their entire childhood in survival mode.

I thought about the brightest moments in my own childhood— they were often simple, like my mom teaching me to shuffle cards, or my dad teaching me to whistle with a blade of grass. I thought about the most treasured moments with my own kids. Many of them were just as simple, and yet nothing like I thought they would be.

I'd pictured special times at our dining table doing crafts together. I didn't realize some of our best memories would instead be made when we gave up on the failed craft and, to escape the house, drove down to eat lunch while watching trains.

I was focused on the end result of activities, like swimming lessons, and didn't realize some of our most precious memories would be made on the way there, looking for the prairie dogs that make their homes in the lot near the city pool.

When I thought parenting had to be perfect like the picture in my head, I hardly could enjoy the "perfectly imperfect" moments that came every day. I had no idea parenting would be so messy, so unpredictable, so freaking tiring. *No idea.* And the harder I held on to how I thought it should be, the worse I felt.

I had to let go to appreciate what was really in front of me. I had to start looking for these simple and sweet moments that were often happening at the same time as the messy and loud moments. That was the first stage in becoming a Bounceback Parent—bouncing back from the disappointment that parenting would not be like the fairy tale in my head.

Overall, it's actually a much richer experience than I had pictured, but before I could see that, I also had to let go and acknowledge some of the pain of it being different.

✎ Field Notes: Edit Your Possibilities

We start out parenting with so much possibility—it's nearly intoxicating to have all those options, so many things to try! We imagine the children we'll have, and then we imagine the childhood we'll make for them.

We see friends taking kids to gymnastics or music lessons; we find books full of activities, story time at the library, soccer clubs, scouts, art classes, and more. Shouldn't we be doing those things too? Can you really be a good parent if you choose only one, or none, of those activities? As our image of the perfect childhood gets tattered and trampled by the realities of parenting, we worry that we're not doing enough.

What we're forgetting is that we're seeing hundreds of possibilities, but it doesn't mean a good childhood has to involve all those things. They are exciting possibilities, but if we worry about all of them, they quickly become suffocating, exhausting, overwhelming—filling us with shoulds and dissatisfaction.

Instead, we're going to take a look at your own family and edit your possibilities to fit what matters most to you. What are the traditions and the moments that mean the most to you? Put your energy there. Remember, it's okay to let it be easy; give yourself permission to let go of some of the things you envisioned, to make room for what's happening now.

When we hold on to too many possibilities, we can't enjoy what is.

Letting Go

What did you imagine parenting to look and feel like? What shocked you about the reality versus your expectations? What made you sad to find out? What joyfully surprised you?

....

....

....

....

....

....

....

....

....

....

....

....

....

....

....

....

....

....

....

Do you have parenting fantasies or imaginings that are getting in the way of noticing the way your family really is? Would you like to let go of any of these ideas?

....

....

....

....

....

....

....

....

....

....

....

....

....

....

....

....

....

....

....

....

....

Mission: Processing Loss, Finding Hope

As you think about letting go, you may notice feelings of sadness or a sense of being "unmoored." When we let go of how we thought things would be, even for the positive reason of being open to what is here in our present life, it can shake our foundations.

For this mission, you'll begin to process the grief of letting go of a treasured dream you had about parenting. Letting go means loss. This is why we grieve—in order to acknowledge the loss, and then let it go. One thing I've learned about grief is that if I can experience the feelings and truly acknowledge them, they become less scary, and I become more whole.

In this mission, you'll counterpoint grief with gratitude to help you process loss and find hope.

✔️ Your Assignment: Write a Letter to the Dream You've Lost

THIS EXERCISE IS DESIGNED TO GENTLY SUPPORT YOUR FEELINGS OF GRIEF AND ALLOW YOU TO ACKNOWLEDGE A LOSS.

Think about dreams you may have had for parenting that you now realize will not come true.

Possibly:

- I will have a boy.
- I will have a girl.
- I'll have more than one child.
- I'll have only one child.
- I didn't plan to have children.
- My child will be healthy.
- My child will love the things I do.
- My child will have a mellow temperament.
- My child will understand how I feel.

- My child will be an A student.
- My child will be a star athlete.
- My child will look a particular way.
- My child will have no problems with mental health.
- I will not yell at my child.
- I will always understand what my child needs.
- I will not repeat mistakes made during my childhood.

Write a letter to that lost dream—whether it's to the daughter you will never have, the family you thought you would have, or the person you thought you would be. No worries about writing with perfect handwriting or beautiful prose; you will not be keeping this letter, so you can feel free to write whatever comes up for you.

In your letter, acknowledge your lost dreams and tell them about the pain of realizing they won't come true. Write about what you hoped for and what you're sad to be missing. It's hard to give up preconceptions and may take some time to come to terms with *what is* instead what you thought *would be.* Know that you are not a bad person for feeling sad or confused. You are experiencing this grief so that you can make some peace with it and be able to focus on what you have now.

Once you've written your letter, it's time to take one more step toward processing this loss. Take your letter and either burn it or, if you prefer, rip it into tiny pieces and throw it away. This is a physical reminder that you're acknowledging a hope and letting it go.

When we grieve what we have lost, even if that loss is the illusion of how we thought family life would be, we honor our hopes and dreams and we make space for new hopes and dreams to come into the world. This lets us begin to be more present for where we are and able to commit to our current reality.

☑ Your Assignment: Capture Gratitude

GRATITUDE HELPS US BUILD UP HOPE AND ENERGY FOR OUR PRESENT REALITY.

For the next five days you're on a mission to capture gratitude through the lens of your camera. Your phone camera is fine. Take a picture each day of something you're grateful for—it could be anything, big or small, from your morning cup of coffee to your child asleep at the end of a long day.

Use a photo collage maker (there are many free programs online) to make a collage of these photos. You can share the collage on Instagram or Facebook, or use it as a computer background or a phone backdrop as a way to remind yourself of your gratitude.

Meeting the Should Mama

Now that you're lighter for having let go of a few of your preconceived notions, and more nimble for having tried on a growth mindset in your parenting, you are ready to confront our chief adversary: the Should Mama.

The Should Mama (or Should Papa) is the nefarious enemy of the Bounceback Parent. She resides inside us, telling us all the things we should be doing. Once you recognize her fearful voice you'll be more aware of when you are bending to her wishes instead of making choices yourself.

This is the story of when I first recognized the Should Mama and the misery she was inflicting on my life.

The Should Mama

It's definitely after midnight when I hear my three-year-old crying. Again.

This isn't one of those times she'll drift back to sleep. It's the third (fourth?) time she's awoken crying. I've been up and down all night—just falling asleep only to be awoken again.

She's got to be sick . . . I don't feel a fever . . . What's going *on*?

I sit by her bed, exhausted, foggy, trying to get her back to sleep, trying to figure out if she's had a nightmare or if she's about to puke in my hair. Perhaps she's getting a cold . . . ?

I'm so tired. I'm pleading, "Please, Zee, Mama is tired, and she wants to go to bed. Can you go back to sleep now? Please?"

And then the guilt starts. (It's 1:00 a.m., do you know where your guilt is?)

> It's 1:00 a.m., do you know where your guilt is?

You know, says the voice in my head . . .

You should stop telling her about how tired you are—it's teaching her to put your needs ahead of her own; she'll think she has to take care of you.

If you were doing this right you'd come up with a story right now to help her fall asleep. She would always remember how kind you were at night. You should be like that.

For that matter, you don't read picture books to her enough. You should read to her more.

For goodness' sake! She fell asleep listening to the Harry Potter book with her brothers. I think maybe you're ruining her toddlerhood. I bet she's crying right now because she's having terrible Harry Potter nightmares.

And look at this room they share!

You should have had them clean before bed—look at her, poor girl, she's taking all her toys onto her bed because she has no clean, tidy space.

Toddlers need order. They crave it. You might be ruining her brain with this mess.

You should get rid of more toys.

You should be telling her a story.

You should get the boys on a better schedule.

You should have made them clean up before bed.

You should have brushed her teeth, not let her do it on her own.

You should teach them better money sense.

You should make them write thank-you notes more quickly.

You should eat dinner at the table every night.

You should . . .

You should . . .

You should . . .

You . . . You know what?

You're probably ruining your kids.

You should . . .

Oh my goodness! I finally snap out of it.

I am squatting, uncomfortably, by my toddler at 1:00 a.m.

And you know what, Should Mama? I haven't lost it! I haven't snapped at her or used an aggravated voice or walked out in a huff to leave her alone. I might not be perfect, but I am being patient and loving and back-rubbing, and I am so *tired*. Really, really danged tired.

I'm doing okay here, and I cannot keep trying to be this Should Mama that my insecurities thrust at me.

I sit in the dark, rubbing my daughter's back. Her perfect little face is finally calm again as she falls asleep, soothed from her discomfort. Safe with her mama's touch.

Me. She needs me. She doesn't want that other mom who always keeps a clean living room and sings like Snow White.

She doesn't waste time comparing me to the Should Mama. She wants *her* mama here being patient in the dark.

She wants *me*.

You know what will ruin my kids? It's not any of those things on the list of shoulds.

What will ruin my kid is if I let all of those shoulds bury the things that make me, me.

In the early hours of the morning I sit in the bedroom of my sleeping children and make a promise to myself:

My kids may not get someone who has schedules down to a science. They may not get the mama who always has fun games for cleanup time. They may not get the birthday-party-perfect mama.

But they *will get me*.

And you know what?

I make really good pancakes.

I can make up a silly jingle for any situation. I know how to do an underdog push on the swing and make a bridge when I shuffle cards, and I can start a conversation with anyone. I can uplift a friend when she's down and make a guest feel comfortable in my home. I find the positive side of a problem, and I find gratitude even in distressing times.

I will not let the Should Mama take all that from my kids. I will not waste all my time comparing myself to her and let her suck the joy out of my parenting.

Oh, I'll keep learning, I'll keep questioning. I will look at those shoulds, but I will not be held hostage by them, because I am somebody right now, and my kids need me.

Right now my kids need *me*.

Field Notes: Who Are *You*?

Who do your kids miss out on when you spend too much time worrying about the shoulds? When we try to appease the Should Mama we wind up struggling, stuck in a fixed mindset (*If I were a good parent I would . . .*), and we lose the opportunity to shine as ourselves.

In a world of social media, where we can see so many things other parents are doing with their families, it's easy to compare ourselves and lose our joy when we forget that we have our own talents and our own story to live out.

Use the following notebook exercise to remember the good and let go of the should.

> Remember the good and let go of the should.

FINDING GOOD: It takes practice to notice what you're doing well. Finish these sentences to help you see who your family misses out on when you get caught up by the shoulds. If it's hard to complete the sentences, ask your kids to help you with the answers.

I'm learning how to: ....

....

I know how to: ....

....

Something people come to me for advice on is: ....

....

I am secretly proud of: ....

....

My kids love when I: ....

....

My kids laugh when I: ....

....

One of the best things about me is: ....

....

———

LETTING GO OF SHOULDS: What shoulds are you struggling with right now? Let the Should Mama loose on the page and write down as many shoulds as you can think of. You may want to take a few days to write this list so that you have time to notice all the shoulds that float through your mind.

....

....

....

....

....

....

....

....

....

....

....

....

....

....

....

....

....

....

....

....

....

....

....

....

....

....

....

....

....

....

Take a look at your list of shoulds. Which ones actually make you feel joy or excitement? Which ones feel heavy, obligatory, or exhausting? Can you let go of any of the shoulds?

Mission: Replace the Shoulds

One more way to keep the Should Mama at bay is to change your words. Instead of shoulds, you can begin noticing coulds. *Could* allows you to be more intentional about what you make room for in your life.

What Should Says

Should says, "You are not enough. You should do X, Y or Z, then you *might* be more deserving." Should puts contentment out of reach and perpetuates the illusion that we will at some point reach a "completed" perfect state when we can enjoy our kids (but not until then!). Truthfully, we are all works in progress and all have room for growth. If we wait until we meet some illusory level of perfection to let ourselves be present and enjoy our kids, we'll miss their childhood.

Let's Try This Instead

Try replacing *should* with *could*, *might*, or *choose to*.

Example:

I should make a better morning routine for our family.

This invokes a sense of weight and "one more thing to do." It reminds you of yet one more place you're supposedly falling short. And because the list of shoulds is unending, it continues the thinking that you will never be enough.

Instead:

I could make a better morning routine for our family.

This invites a sense of possibility. It reminds you that you have choices. You can choose to do this, but you also might not choose to do this right now. *Could* moves us into a more proactive mindset where we are empowered to make or discard a choice.

✅ Your Assignment: Replacing *Should* with *Could*

Next time you realize you're "shoulding" on yourself . . . catch yourself and try substituting the word *could* instead.

🚩 Want to post a reminder for yourself? Check in the archives at online headquarters for a printable poster that will remind you to stop shoulding on yourself.

🕵️ Mission: Decision Making with a Growth Mindset

Alert! Your Should Mama embodies the fixed mindset. She doesn't let you see that for many choices in life there is more than one "right" answer.

She tells you: if you make a choice that results in struggle, you're doing it wrong. The Should Mama is fearful of making wrong choices so she overwhelms us with things we "should" do to get things "right." She holds the mistaken belief that if we make all the right choices, everything will be easy.

Changing this belief (and noticing when I'm slipping back into it) has been key to becoming less anxious and more present in my life.

Opportunities for Growth

When I was a kid I would agonize over decisions. I wanted to go to the birthday party with my friends but still have dinner with my dad. I wanted to go to the movies but also stay home and play a game. Couldn't we do both—isn't there a way to fit it all in? I'd be in tears, sure I was going to choose wrong and miss out.

When I became a parent, this type of thinking spread worry throughout my days. Whether about fun activities or life-changing decisions, I constantly worried I was making the wrong choice. Should I nurse the baby to sleep or set him down in bed? Should we use the backless booster or the convertible car seat? Should we homeschool or send them to school? Should we have Easter with grandparents or stay home? I constantly looked for reassurance that I was right. I was stuck in the Should Mama mindset that there was only one right path.

I spent a lot of time being half present because I constantly looked back, analyzing whether I'd made the right choice. I frequently felt sad or guilty that things didn't work out smoothly. In my fixed-mindset state, I thought challenges indicated I was making all the wrong choices.

So what has changed? How have I stopped rehashing the past so much and freed myself for future decisions?

One day I realized all choices have crappy consequences.

What?

Well, maybe I ought to show you the actual quote from my wise friend Amy Cichan. She said:

I think it is important to remember that all *choices lead to hardship. Life is hard. It will continue to kick you around. But you also get to continue to find ways to move through these temporary conditions. "If only" you had chosen another path, you would be presented with a different set of crappy things. I find this line of thinking to be freeing. When you let go of believing that you are in control of everything and that if you make all the right choices only good things will happen, you are no longer responsible for all misery and you can focus on dealing with the current temporary condition instead of beating yourself up about having made the wrong choice.*

When we realize we are not doing it wrong if we struggle, it is indeed freeing. And in fact, what's happening is that we're moving into the growth mindset.

- Instead of believing we need to control everything to have a family life free of challenges, we can see challenges as opportunities for growing together.
- Instead of believing we have to make our kids happy, we can see opportunities for them to grow more resilient.
- Instead of believing others are doomed to fail, we can look for their strengths and see opportunities for them to build on that foundation.

Letting go of the notion that right choices create a life without challenges empowers us to stop being so hard on ourselves and start seeing opportunities for growth.

✏️ Field Notes: Moving Forward

Sometimes we never really know if we made the right choice. Do you have choices that haunt you? Is it time to finish your rehashing and reconsidering of a choice that you've made in the past? What can you do to accept your choice and move forward from where you are now?

....

....

....

....

....

....

....

....

....

....

....

....

....

....

....

....

....

....

....

Debriefing

Congratulations on completing the first level of training for the Bounceback Parenting League!

During this training:

- You've learned that you can enjoy less guilt and more empowerment when you parent with a growth mindset—meaning you believe everyone can improve their abilities through effort and time, starting from right where they are.
- You've begun letting go of how you thought parenting would be; you can see your family more clearly and have more realistic expectations.
- You've learned to recognize the Should Mama or Should Papa in your head who holds you back from who you *could* be, keeping you distracted with too many expectations of how you should parent and preventing you from embracing who you are.
- And now that you know about the growth mindset, you're able to see opportunities for growth when making choices, even if you're uncertain about the choice.

More to Explore

- What messages would you give yourself as a new mom or dad about the growth mindset and parenting? (Such as: It's normal not to have the answers; we're all growing and learning.) Do you think you would have believed them?

- Have you ever hidden something you've done as a parent, fearing it would show others that you are actually a "bad parent"? What do you believe about this incident now?

- What is occurring in your life right now that is not like you thought it would be?

- Where do you think your shoulds come from?

- Think back to a time you agreed to do something that was a "heck *yeah* I want to do this!" type of event for you. Maybe it was difficult or inconvenient, but you were thrilled to do it anyway. How did that feel? What happened?

- Describe a time you agreed to do something that was only a should—not a "heck yeah" but an "I guess I should." How does it feel when you're saying yes: How does your body feel, your thoughts; what do you tell yourself that makes you say yes? How does it feel when you're doing the task?

- Some choices feel impossible—impossible to let go of something, impossible to choose between priorities. Are you facing a choice like this? What will you lose if you don't choose? Is this a time when it will be okay to wait on making a choice? Do you think you have a fixed mindset (like there is one right answer) about this choice?

....

....

....

....

....

....

....

....

....

....

....

....

....

....

....

....

....

....

....

....

....

....

....

....

....

....

....

....

....

....

....

....

....

....

....

....

....

....

....

....

....

CHAPTER THREE

Operation Everyday Connection

Message from Ops

Bounceback Parenting HQ has discovered that the Should Mama has been up to her usual tricks—sending messages to overwhelm parents. She's been broadcasting a long list of all the things that make someone a "good parent." But forget all that. We're going to simplify with Operation Everyday Connection. When your priorities are clear, it's easier to make choices as a parent. Your connected relationship with your child is top priority.

The Should Mama would like you to think connection is out of your reach, that you're doing it wrong. She wants to tell you all the things you "should" be doing to have a truly connected family. However, she tends to exaggerate things a bit. The Should Mama might say you need to volunteer for all the school events, throw expensive birthday parties, and go on fancy vacations to theme parks. These can be opportunities to connect, but the Should Mama is wrong when she tells you they're requirements.

In *Connection Parenting*, Pam Leo writes, "What our children need most, money can't buy. Our children need human connection. A healthy, strong parent-child bond, created through consistent, loving connection, is essential to our children's wellbeing and optimal development. This bond is also the key to our effectiveness as parents."

During Operation Everyday Connection we'll first get an understanding of why connection matters, then we'll find out why it's easier to build a connected relationship than the Should Mama has led you to believe. You'll finish this operation knowing practical and simple ways you can add connection to your everyday life.

Why Connection Matters

Simply put, connection makes everything else easier.

> Connection makes everything else easier.

Children who feel connected want to follow their parents' lead. Connection makes facing challenges together easier because we trust one another, and when we practice connection every day, we increase the resilience of our relationships. That resilience gives you the ability to reconnect after you've suffered a break in your relationship, allowing you to "bounce back" and increase the strength of your bond with your child.

Connection becomes a self-fulfilling prophecy—something that builds on itself. If you've ever faced a challenge with a team, you know the good feeling that can come out of succeeding together. Our families have this same potential—and then some.

Connection Carries You Through the Hard Parts

It was summer and my husband, three kids, two dogs, and I were driving in our VW bus from our home in Arizona up to a campground near Yosemite. This was a long-awaited trip. For the first time in years both my husband and I had twelve days off together; the kids had been talking excitedly about meeting their grandparents at the lake, and my husband had spent weeks working on the bus to make sure it was ready for the trip. We had snacks, games, and a sense of adventure about the nine-hour drive. The only thing we were a little worried about was crossing Death Valley in the summer without air conditioning—we figured as long as we didn't get stuck out there, the trip would be great.

The drive was going as planned until, you guessed it, the bus shuddered to a stop—in Death Valley. We were almost a hundred miles from the nearest town. If there was ever a middle of nowhere, we'd found it. All that preparation and anticipation, and there we were, stuck on the side of the freeway in 119°F heat. When we called for a tow truck, the nearest one could reach us in three hours.

We settled in to wait, using the combination of water bottles and fans we'd brought along to cool ourselves down.

This "adventure" called on our connection as a family. "Okay, kids, you know how we talk about going above and beyond in our family? This is one of those times when we really need to go above and beyond to be kind and calm." The kids could sense that their dad felt terrible about the bus breaking down, and instead of complaining they did their best to make the situation better by offering him water and inviting him to play a game of Uno. This simple act of connection allowed us to get through the long wait in the heat, an eighty-five-mile drive in a tow truck, and hours in the parking lot of an auto parts store.

At the end of this long day we finally found a motel (with a pool!). My kids were thrilled to go swimming, and months later our youngest even asked to go back to that motel and pool in Barstow because it was "such a fun day"! What could have been a disaster turned into a memory-making family adventure.

This was possible *not* because we instinctively knew how to be connected during this difficult day, but because we practice connecting in our ordinary days through simple interactions like talking, playing, and doing chores together. The connection built during these everyday experiences in our family carried us through what could have been a terrible part of our trip and made it into a great memory. The kids remember this experience because there wasn't any yelling, and there was a pool at the end. We as parents remember it because it was a day in which we really saw the rewards of practicing connection.

✎ Field Notes: What Connection Means to You

- What does it feel like when you're connected with your kids?

....

....

....

....

....

....

....

....

....

- What is your biggest struggle with connecting with your kids?

....

....

....

....

....

....

....

....

....

....

....

....

....

....

- List at least three tiny connection moments that might happen during your ordinary day (for instance, talking in the car, sharing your favorite part of the day during dinner, or giving goodnight kisses).

....

....

....

....

....

....

....

....

- Name three bigger "events" that increase connection in your family (for instance, going camping together, having a family game night, going out to lunch with one of your kids).

....

....

....

....

....

....

....

....

....

Connection, Not Perfection

Our goal for Operation Everyday Connection is to reset your connection meter so that you can see the connection that already happens with your kids and notice opportunities to connect that you may
have dismissed as "not enough" before. Use the phrase "connection,
not perfection" to remember that circumstances don't
have to be perfect—and people don't have to be
perfect—to build resilient, connected relationships.

**Connection, not
perfection.**

The practice of connection is part of life—both ups
and downs.

Connection is a combination of presence and acceptance; it's made
up of everyday moments when we turn *toward* instead of *away*. Frequently we think of connection as being happy and snuggly with the
people we love, but it's more than those cozy moments. Here are examples of more nuanced expressions of connection.

- Connection happens when we're grieving and sharing memories
  about someone we cared for who has died.
- Connection happens when we're vulnerable with one another,
  share a part of ourselves that we fear to reveal, and find acceptance.

- Connection happens when we really listen to each other's stories and accept the other person's experience and feelings, even if those differ from our own.

Connection is a choice we make over and over again—in joyful moments and sad, in fearful times and loving. It is the nutrient that allows for growth, and it is the strongest influence parents have over children.

Connection in families ebbs and flows—sometimes we get busy or distracted, or life circumstances throw a wrench in the works. When connection is at a low, the usual indicator is that everything gets harder. People are less forgiving with one another and more likely to see the other's faults. This means connection is the first thing to check up on when you have a child who is acting out; it is where to look when you're feeling frustrated or upset with one of your kids, and it is where to look when you're feeling anxious about your child. Ask yourself: How is our connection lately? Do they need a little more attention from me?

It's All About Practice

The Should Mama may tell us that connection only happens when we make time for one-on-one play, or during special events like going out to lunch or on a trip together—but those are only the events.

Connection is more of a practice. Connection is a part of everyday life through the way you interact during mundane tasks like making lunches, reviewing homework together, or waiting at the dentist. As my brother says, "Ninety percent of relationship is in showing up and just doing life together."

When you stop looking at connection as a special event and instead think of it as a practice, you see that you have countless practice opportunities.

You Can Find Connection

In the way you greet the people you love
and the way you say goodbye.

In having curiosity, listening openly,
and seeing your child as a person who can contribute to the conversation.

In pausing to do something at your child's pace,
even when it doesn't feel convenient.

In the moment you take a deep breath and give a true apology,
letting your child see you are vulnerable.

And any time you laugh together.

The practice of connection may include something big, like a birthday party or a graduation celebration, but it is practiced more frequently in day-to-day interactions when we notice the moment just as it is, and the people who are with us—whole and loved, just as they are.

Connection isn't about getting all these things right. The truth is, building connection and trust into our family lives will look different for each of us. It's not about neglecting your own needs or doing only what your kids want. It's about finding the ways to connect that work in your family and transforming your days by trying these ways to connect over and over again.

Connection is a practice, not an event.

Mission: Smile to Be More Present

It's easy to get caught up in the busyness of our days. Especially if your family is feeling disconnected right now, it may be overwhelming thinking about the work you need to do to connect again.

Thankfully there is a powerful yet tiny step you can take today that makes a huge difference.

It is the simple practice of smiling. In her book *MOMfulness*, Denise Roy calls smiling "mouth yoga."

Try it today.

Smile when your child walks into the room. Smile when you hear your child laugh. And smile at some time when you're just going along in your day (I usually remember when I'm driving). Smiling has a marvelous way of bringing you present, and when we are present we are connected—to ourselves, our life, and our kids.

[Smiling] won't get the dishes done any faster or create less laundry for us to do. What smiling will do is remind us that underneath all of our busyness, there's grace, there's a spaciousness that we can bring inside of us. It reminds us that in this moment, we are well. Perhaps we'll be surprised to discover

ourselves being grateful for the soapy water, for the noisy kids in the back-seat. Perhaps in that moment we will find peace.

—*DENISE ROY,* MOMFULNESS

☑ Your Assignment: Smile

Today practice smiling when your child walks into the room. Your smile says, "I'm grateful to have you in my life."

Mission: Adding Connection to Daily Rituals

The way we think about mundane daily interactions becomes import-ant when we're looking for everyday connection. It might feel weighty to think *every moment counts*, but for me, it feels like free-dom. It gives me permission to find connection during the most rou-tine tasks, like tying a shoe or planning what to buy at the grocery store. Taking advantage of the ability to connect during these every-day moments takes the pressure off special events for connection.

The first place I looked to make connection part of our daily ritu-als was at the beginning of our day.

The Best Way to Start a Day

The best advice I ever received about starting my day as a parent was not "Get up before your kids do." It was "Be doing something that can be interrupted." Before taking that bit of advice to heart, I would often find myself frustrated and resentful when my quiet morning was interrupted and I had to pause in the middle of writing or other concentrated work. I wanted to give the kids a smile and a snuggle first thing, but it was a lot harder to smile when I was feeling resentful about the interruption. This changed with a simple mental shift.

I still write frequently in the morning, but now if I'm up before the kids I try to choose what's most important to work on first (avoiding the "Ack! I just wasted all that time on Facebook!" feeling) and then I work while keeping in mind that I may be interrupted soon. It feels like any work that gets done is a bonus. I want my kids to have years' worth of memories of being greeted not with an attitude that says, "Oh, crud, you again," but instead says, "Hello! I'm so glad you're in my life. How lucky we get to share this day together!"

Small shifts in our thinking or actions like this form positive connection rituals in our families.

In *I Love You Rituals*, Becky Bailey highlights the power of everyday connection: "Rituals are love moments. They are the moments in life when all else stops and we take time to reconnect with each other and remember who we are—loving caring beings. Rituals can serve us well during transitions during a busy day."

EXAMPLES OF EVERYDAY CONNECTION RITUALS IN OUR FAMILY

- Giving the kids a hug and a smile when they wake up in the morning
- Waving enthusiastically from the driveway when someone leaves

- Saying silly things like "Home again home again jiggity jig" when we're on our way home
- Asking at dinnertime, "What was your favorite part of the day?"
- Watching our favorite show all together on the couch
- Celebrating birthdays by starting the day with dutch baby pancakes and bacon for breakfast, and hanging up a birthday banner
- Putting lavender in our woodstove steamer on winter evenings
- Making tea and a snuggle spot on the couch for a sick family member
- Having good-night rituals for each of the kids: one of our sons likes having his back scratched and a kiss on the cheek, the other prefers a quick hug, and our daughter often likes roughhousing "upside-down snuggles" from my husband yet wants to be tucked in and kissed on each cheek from me

In short, rituals help us gain the habit of being connected and present with the most important people in our lives. They are the simple sounds, scents, and experiences that make up the unique feeling of home in your family. Looking at the way your day already flows gives you a chance to intentionally add a few more connection rituals to your ordinary routines.

✔ Your Assignment: Morning Snuggles

A morning I-love-you ritual is a simple way to start the day well. When you first see your child in the morning, stop whatever you're doing, smile, and give a hug. You don't have to spend fifteen minutes snuggling (though go for it if that works for you)—just beginning your day with a quick hug and smile feels good. In our family, we call these morning snuggles—and I love this ritual because it starts us off positively. I know that whatever else comes our way for the day, at least I've set out on the right foot. My kids have even asked for morning snuggles in the middle of the afternoon if we somehow managed to forget them!

✏️ Field Notes: Take a Needs Inventory

One of the things that gets in the way of connecting is when we can't understand where our kids are coming from. Bonnie Harris observes in her book *Confident Parents, Remarkable Kids* that acceptance of our children is more powerful even than love, because it is our acceptance of our kids as whole people that allows us to connect with them and help them grow into their best selves.

Whenever I realize I'm feeling at odds with one of my kids, it usually indicates I've lost track of where they are in their life at that moment and I'm only seeing things from my perspective. Kids grow and change; it's normal to get out of sync sometimes. To reconnect, I need to gain deeper insight into why they're behaving the way they are and what they might need.

When I look at things from my child's perspective, I can let go of some of my frustration and find compassion instead. Compassion arises from understanding. If you're having a hard time connecting with one of your children in particular, I suggest you prioritize doing this exercise with that child in mind. To regain understanding, fill out the needs inventory for your child.

In his Five Love Languages books, Gary Chapman explains that we all have different things that make us feel loved. If we express love in the other person's "love language," they are more likely to feel loved. The following questions are inspired by his books.

Use these questions to recalibrate as you and your child grow and change over time. Take the questions lightly—if you're struggling to answer one, leave it and let the question sit in your mind as you go through your day; it will tune your awareness toward your child, helping you see what he or she needs right now.

NEEDS INVENTORY

What makes this child feel loved? (Touch? Conversation? Doing activities together?) *Write down a few specific examples—then keep your eye out for more, or ask your child for ideas.*

....

....

....

....

....

....

....

....

....

What activities or family jobs allow this child's unique skills to shine? How can I remind this child he or she is valuable to the family? (For instance, one of my kids shines when asked to help plan our meals, while another shines when asked to help care for the animals.)

....

....

....

....

....

....

....

If all my actions say one sentence to this child, what should that sentence be? (For instance, one of my kids may need to see and hear "I'm stable and safe for you." And another, "I want to know you just as you are.")

....

....

....

....

....

What do I want to enjoy about this child right now? (The way he or she laughs? His or her joy about a certain book? The way he or she runs?) *What do you want to remember to savor?*

....

....

....

....

....

....

How does this child act when he or she needs love but doesn't know how to tell me? (Getting demanding? Toilet accidents? Being overly silly? Headaches? Angry outbursts?) *What behavior or symptom is a clue that his or her emotional cup needs filling?*

....

....

....

....

....

....

Visit the archives in our online headquarters to print more of these journal pages at bouncebackparenting.com/HQ.

Better Communication for
Better Everyday Connection

The easiest way to bring more connection to your family life is through becoming a better communicator. For me, that started with listening better.

It's More Than the Legos

We stood in my friend's kitchen, chatting and drinking coffee, when one of her sons walked in and said, "Hey, look what I made!"

We politely listened and oohed and aahed as he gave a detailed description of the Lego spaceship with all the bells and whistles. We'd been chatting quite a while, as moms do, and I think we both felt like he needed this moment to have our attention, but when he left the room I told her that sometimes it's so hard for me to listen to Lego descriptions or other seemingly never-ending conversation topics from my kids. My constant phrase seemed to be "Not right now!" or rushing them to finish up their description.

She said, "I have a hard time too, but I want them to know that I will listen to them when they have something important to tell me. Right now it's Legos, but what about a few years from now? It could be drugs or sex. I want them to feel like they can talk to me, and if I don't show them that I value their interests now, why would they turn to me later when the topics get even more difficult or uncomfortable?"

Wow—if I hadn't been motivated before, suddenly it became very clear to me that the channels of open communication I set up now would be critical later.

These little moments of listening were smoothing the way for long-term deep connection. I started seeing the commentary on Lego spaceships as an invitation into their world.

On the other hand, I got better about saying, "I'm not able to focus on this right now, but how about we talk at bedtime (or while I make dinner, or when we're driving to the store . . .)," and then making sure I paid attention when I said I would. Ten minutes of my focus is one hundred times better than an hour of partial attention and annoyance.

Along with getting better about noticing when I was totally distracted while "listening," I began looking at how I shut down communication by jumping in too quickly or being uncomfortable about a topic. My husband and I both gradually improved our ability to listen during seemingly trivial conversations.

The benefit of these small conversations is the habits they form between family members. My oldest now seeks out "Papa time" after the other two kids are in bed. These conversations are important as he enters middle school and faces new complexities in his life. We keep the door open to them through the small moments of conversation that are about more than "just the Legos."

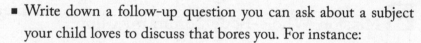

Field Notes: Get the Conversation Started

- Write down a specific time you will try to start a conversation this week (such as on the way to school, before bed, while waiting in line, etc.).

....

....

....

- Write down a follow-up question you can ask about a subject your child loves to discuss that bores you. For instance:
  - What do you think would make _____ even better?
  - What's the most surprising thing you've learned recently about _____?
  - What makes you the most excited about _____?

  Write your own follow-up question here.

....

....

....

- Sometimes you truly can't listen. It's much easier to stay kind if we practice another response besides, "*Shush!* Enough!" Plan a gracious exit to a conversation. For instance:
  - That sounds like something your friend _____ would love to hear more about.

- ◆ I'm losing focus right now, can we discuss this again [at this time]?
- ◆ Hang on, I need to _____ first before I can fully listen.

Can you think of a way to respectfully yet clearly end a conversation? Write it here.

....

....

....

Mission: Whole-Body Communication

Whole-body communication—what does that mean? It's about making the choice to communicate with your child and be there in that moment with your full self when possible (obviously we've got to keep eyes on the road while driving and that sort of thing).

First, it helps your child recognize what it looks and feels like to be fully listened to. As they learn what it's like to have someone listen to them, they'll gain a better understanding of when their message is getting across. In our household I'm known to say, "Wait, give me a couple of minutes to finish this; I want to give you my full attention when you're talking to me," and because they know what it means to get my full attention, they're more willing to wait (sometimes we set a timer too, so they have a visual reference).

Another reason I practice this kind of listening is because I want my children to grow up expecting to be respected, and choosing life partners with whom they can communicate and grow. I believe that when I model good listening, they will see it as the norm and seek it out in others, making it more likely that they will be surrounded by people who communicate with respect and presence.

This is an ongoing dance—the more I give them whole-body communication, the more they are able to be patient when I need them to and the more they offer respect.

How to Listen with Your Whole Self

- If you answer a question while you're at the computer, where are your hands? Where is your body facing—the computer or your child?
- If you want your child to do something, and you're explaining it to them, where are you? Are you near your child? Are you by his or her side or calling from another room?
- If they're calling you from another room, can you invite your child to come to you instead of trying to talk across the house?
- If your child doesn't listen the first time you ask him or her to do something, can you try a respectful physical touch to focus attention? For instance, you might put your hand on your child's arm or shoulder while you talk.
- If you're looking at your phone and your child asks you a question, do you shift your gaze? What about your phone—is it still glowing in front of you, or is it placed facedown on the table or tucked in a pocket?
- If you can't listen right now, what do you need to do? Is it a matter of placing a bookmark in your novel, clicking "save" on

computer work, or letting them know you need a moment before you can devote full attention?

Whole-body communication takes a lot of practice, and the reality is you're not going to be able to do this perfectly all the time—sometimes I get entangled in three conversations at once simply because I have three kids, and we're all still working on becoming more patient people. The point is to practice whole-body communication as much as you can.

✔️ Your Assignment: Listening Practice

When you're talking to your children today, check to see whether you're listening and communicating with your whole body—you're in the same room, you're looking at them, and your body is facing them.

🕵️ Mission: Ten Minutes of Special Time

Kids who feel connected to their parents are more able to grow, learn, and be their best selves.

All children (all people, actually) want to do the right thing and will do so as long as they can. If the child is not in a receptive state, she will not learn. In other words, she must want to learn and hear what is being taught.
—BONNIE HARRIS

Before a child will be receptive to what you want to teach, he or she needs connection to you. Children need the safety to be themselves and risk making mistakes as they learn.

We can connect with kids through acceptance and presence, and—good news—short amounts of time make a big difference. I learned about this first from Amy McCready, a positive-parenting expert, who calls it "mind, body, and soul time." We call it "special time"; my friend's family calls it "you-and-me time." Whatever you call this time together, it's one-on-one time with your child.

Special time is a simple concept with big results, and, happily, it doesn't even require boatloads of patience. I recommend starting with putting aside ten minutes to connect with your child—no phones or other distractions for that chunk of time. Follow your child's lead to the extent that you can. You may wish to set out a few ideas at the beginning, such as games you know you both enjoy. **Connection, not perfection reminder!** It doesn't have to be perfect. Try for connection, not perfection. With three kids, multiple pets, and the unpredictability that can bring, special time gets interrupted here sometimes. Also, while it would be ideal if I could do special time every day, the truth is I rarely manage to do it with each of them every day. Even when I keep it up sporadically and imperfectly, they love special time, and our relationship feels closer because of it. If you've got one child in particular who is out of sorts, make the priority to do special time with him or her if no one else.

How Can Just Ten Minutes Together Have an Impact?

Maybe sometimes you can plan for more, but ten minutes is a great way to start. The short time period is what makes special time so powerful. We can find ten minutes in our day. We can focus for ten minutes. We can listen to conversations about Minecraft or My Little Pony for that short period of time. For ten minutes we can be patient and present, and our kids thrive in our presence.

Ten minutes is enough to get you started and give you moments of connection with your children that lead you to want to create those moments more often. When you've had a terrible week and you feel angry or resentful, ten minutes is enough to begin bridging the gap that has occurred between you and your child. When you regularly connect one-on-one with each of your kids, you will begin to know what really makes each child feel loved as an individual—and you can do this just ten minutes at a time.

✅ Your Assignment: Seek Out Special Time

Build your connection by doing ten minutes of special time with whichever child you're most wanting to bond with right now. If you're feeling worried, guilty, exasperated, or at a loss with one of your kids, special time can be a healing balm. It's the place to start.

✏️ Field Notes: Our Favorite Easy Activities

One of the biggest blocks to spending time with your kids isn't actually time. It feels like time is the issue, but usually we could find five or ten minutes here and there. We just need to know how to make great use of that time together. What makes it easier is to have a handful of activities at the ready. For this notebook exercise, you're going to write down five activities that you and your kids like to do together and that don't require a lot of preparation from you.

IDEAS FOR YOUR EASY ACTIVITIES LIST

- Ask for company while you do a household chore like folding laundry or doing dishes. Invite your child to chat while you do a task that isn't high stress for you, so you still have patience to chat with your child.
- Chat at bedtime. Reserve ten minutes to talk with your child at the end of the day. If you have multiple children, it can feel special to tuck everyone in, then sneak out to chat in the living room with just one kid after the others have gone to bed, or, if you're exhausted in the evening, maybe it works for one of your kids to snuggle with you for ten minutes first thing in the morning.
- Go on a walk or a run together.
- Draw, color, write in a journal, or paint together.
- Create with Play-Doh or clay.
- Play a board game or card game. Which ones do you both like?

- Read a book aloud. Or, for older children, read the same book separately and grab ten minutes to chat about it.
- Ask a fun conversation-starter question while you're on the way to school.
- Sing or play music together.
- Play with a building toy, or if your child wants to be in charge, help retrieve supplies as he or she needs them.
- Listen to an audiobook together—you might enjoy coloring, finger knitting, or other handwork while listening.
- Make a fort.
- Brush the dog.
- Do arts and crafts.

Stick with activities you don't feel much resistance to doing. You can save more extensive activities for when you have the energy and larger blocks of time. The connection activities on your list are the ones you easily say yes to.

You can find a printable page for this field notes exercise in the archives at our online headquarters. Write down your ideas and put the list on your fridge or keep a list on your phone. When you're feeling frazzled and the kids need attention, look at the list for ideas. You don't always have to come up with a fresh activity—sometimes the old favorites are perfect. It's about the connection and special time spent together—not the activity itself.

Easy Activities for Special Time

Debriefing

By connecting with your children in smaller, daily interactions and practicing connection, not perfection, you have foiled the Should Mama's nefarious plans of allowing only "perfect" interactions and are forming a stronger bonded family through everyday connections.

You gained these valuable insights from Operation Everyday Connection:

- **Connection is a practice, not an event.** If you connect during everyday occurrences, you will be able to weather hard times better and enjoy celebrations in a more connected way.
- **Daily rituals weave connection into your life.** These don't have to be outside of your daily tasks—they might include things like smiling when your child walks in the room, asking about his or her favorite part of the day at dinner, or chatting in the car as you drive.
- **Listening to your kids is one of the most powerful everyday-connection habits you can build.**
  - You can practice whole-body communication by turning toward your children and being present when they're talking.
  - You can listen just a bit longer to the conversation topics that are important to your kids, even if they aren't exciting to you.
  - Making a habit of listening to the everyday stuff means you're ready for those important conversations that come up when you least expect them.
- **Ten minutes is a small amount of time and means the world to your child.** Special time with your child helps you build

connection or reconnect when you feel the need to repair the relationship.

More to Explore

- Can you remember an activity or chore from your childhood that you loved, that the adults around you probably perceived as "just one more to-do" or "nothing special"? Can you think of any chores or activities like this in your family now, during which your kids are probably making good memories?
- What makes you feel loved?
- Are the things that make people in your family feel loved the same things that make you feel loved, or are they different? How do you think this affects the way you communicate with each other?
- Do you think you ever replace connection or presence with gifts or giving in to requests from your kids out of guilt? How does it make you feel later, and how does it affect your connection together?
- Visualize: How would you like your relationship to develop with your children over the next year? Describe how you talk together, how you feel in the same room together, and what they'll remember about interacting with you from this year.

....

....

....

....

....

....

....

....

....

....

....

....

....

....

....

....

....

....

....

CHAPTER FOUR

Operation Compassionate Self-Care

MESSAGE FROM OPS

Alert! Reports from HQ alert us that the Should Mama has been at work again making parents' lives miserable by robbing them of basic necessities like sleep, water, and food, not to mention companionship and fresh air. She was last seen in company of Guilt, lecturing parents that their needs should never come first.

Effective immediately, Ops directs all field agents of the Bounce-back Parenting League to carry out a crucial mission: Operation Compassionate Self-Care.

Our ability to bounce back and be connected parents relies on practicing self-care as part of the process. Practicing self-care means being able to identify your own needs and take steps to tend to them. In Operation Compassionate Self-Care you will learn the basics of self-care that you can do even if your days are busy.

We'll begin to change your mindset about self-care so that you have less resistance to doing it. And you'll learn to trust yourself more as you practice a healthier balance between caring for others and caring for yourself.

Self-Care and Making an Uneasy Truce with Guilt

I thought I would start this chapter talking about why we all deserve self-care. I thought I was going to try to help people not feel guilty about practicing self-care . . . but then I realized something.

I don't know if I will ever stop feeling guilty about taking care of myself.

Self-care means identifying your own needs mentally, emotionally, and physically, and taking steps to meet those needs. That makes sense, right? Yet no matter how much my logical brain says, "You deserve care. We lose our ability to nurture others when we do not nurture ourselves," my emotional brain still says things like, "Maybe if you'd have prepared better you wouldn't need help right now," and "You are only valuable when you're caring for others." It then, unhelpfully, follows up with "Aren't you being a little selfish? After all, they're only little once."

Even though I've come to a place of realizing that taking care of myself is the only way for me to be the kind of mom I want to be (the kind of mom who is mostly able to stay calm, laugh more, and have energy to play with my kids), I still face a twinge of guilt about self-care.

Instead of getting rid of that guilt completely I've reached a different solution. Guilt and I have come to an uneasy truce. I accept that sometimes I will feel guilty, and I can take care of myself anyway.

I tell myself things like, "We all have needs. It's human to have needs," and "You can't pour from an empty vessel." These phrases are mildly helpful in getting past guilt.

I have a pretty strong habit of feeling guilty and then shirking self-care, so sometimes I need more of a kick in the seat of the pants.

When the guilty inner monologue starts up, I have to be honest with myself and accept that if I want to function, I have to recognize and take care of my own needs.

I might ask myself, "Do you want to be dealing with three wild kids and feel like crap too? No? Then first things first: drink water, eat food."

Or I might have to say to myself, "Look, you know you need time to yourself to stay sane and not be a jerk, so let's get on with it."

Yup, I still feel a twinge of guilt. But I can practice doing self-care anyhow.

As one Bounceback Parenting League member told me:

> *When my children were younger I never needed to feel guilty about having self-care because I did not honor myself with any, so instead I felt guilty about being an angry parent who was frazzled and living on my wits end, sleep-deprived and stressed. I know I'd much rather feel guilty about having a quiet cup of tea or doing a short meditation than being an angry short-tempered mom.*

Instead of deciding we need to be perfect about self-care, how about we take a growth mindset about it? We're always learning, and we can be compassionate toward ourselves as we learn more about meeting our own needs. We can get better at self-care with effort and time.

Much like connection, it's about practice.

Field Notes: Reminders of Why Self-Care Matters

Let's get motivated! Use this page to remember why it's crucial to take care of yourself. It's easy to think you can put yourself at the bottom of the list, until you make it obvious to yourself why that has to change. Use the following journal prompts to remind yourself why self-care matters.

> *I had to realize that I was never really going to feel totally worthy of self-care, but I had to start taking care of myself, for my physical health. I guess part of my guilt has been eased by the idea that I have to take care of myself so that I can take care of my kids. I am no good to them or anyone else in the mental state and physical shape I was in. I felt guilty about not being able to be the mom I wanted to be because of my health. . . . I knew I had to do something. I cannot say that I am even halfway up the mountain of taking care of myself, but I have begun the climb.*
>
> —BOUNCEBACK PARENTING LEAGUE MEMBER

Why I Need Self-Care

What happens when you always put yourself last? Who suffers? How do you feel?

- Mentally: Do you get more scattered? Have trouble planning your days?
- Physically: Do you ever get sick when you could stay well if you got enough sleep or nutrients? Have you ever suffered an ongoing health problem from stress?
- Emotionally: Do you get more irritable? Depressed? Resentful or angry?

Write down as many reasons as you can think of why you need to take care of yourself.

....

....

....

....

....

....

....

....

....

....

....

....

....

....

....

....

....

....

....

Mission: HALT for REST

The basics of self-care are identifying your needs and taking steps to tend to them, and REST gives you an action plan. We've got to take care of the basics so that we have enough energy and clarity of mind to function in our families.

When you're in constant caregiver mode, sometimes you forget how to be a caregiver for yourself. You get used to looking after everyone else's needs, and you become numb to your own. That's why we start with REST.

On a good day, you still need these essentials.

On a bad day, you probably need them even more.

If you're feeling hopeless, frantic, fearful, exhausted, or simply unsure what to do next, REST is where to start.

Use these acronyms to remember your next steps. You can do these things even if you're accompanied by guilt and worry.

- **HALT**—If anyone is Hungry, Angry, Lonely, or Tired, they can't function very well. These are the *first* priorities to take care of for yourself and for your kids.

How to take care of these needs?

- Use **REST**. The word says it all:

Rehydrate: Drink a glass of water. See if the kids need water.

Eat: Have you eaten within the last four hours? Get a snack if you need one, then give the kids a snack.

Step (outside): Have you seen the sky today? Stood barefoot on the earth? Stretched? Emotion follows motion—take a walk if you need to. Get the kids outside and moving if they've been indoors all day.

Talk (to someone): Talking with someone reminds us that we're not alone and helps us process difficult emotions. You can call a friend, share in a supportive online group, or call a free parent helpline. It's okay to put kids in front of a movie so that you can catch a little break and get re-centered. If talking with someone else is not a possibility right now, you might try journaling. The act of writing can help distance us from our thoughts enough to gain perspective.

REST: If you're sleep-deprived, nap if possible. Even just ten minutes helps. If a nap is not possible, realize that lack of sleep increases feelings of hopelessness, anxiety, and irritation. Be gentle on yourself and hang in there. Once you get sleep it will be easier to handle daily stresses; for now, just get through today.

✔️ Your Assignment: REST

When the going gets tough—start with REST. Begin by fortifying yourself so you can accomplish the next task more easily. You don't have to take an hour-long break. Get a drink of water. Make sure you have food. Stretch. You are better able to handle a challenge if your basic needs are met.

🚩 Visit HQ online for printable reminders to HALT for REST.

Self-Care Is Not a Reward, It's Part of the Process

"We will never be done. You just have to decide to stop," my husband said after I explained that I was "just trying to catch up" by doing housework late one Saturday evening after the kids had gone to bed.

"I'm always last on the list, if I'm on the list at all," one mom told me, when I asked about self-care. Even though logically we know it's important to take care of ourselves, sometimes we act like rest or basic nourishment are rewards, only for those who've checked off the rest of the to-do list.

This all-too-common line of thinking works something like this:

- Once I have the house clean, then I'll eat lunch. (Never mind that you're actually really hungry right now and having lunch would probably get you working more efficiently.)
- I'd like to read a novel again, but I don't even read aloud enough to the kids, so it would be selfish. (Never mind that reading

makes you feel sane and alive, making you a lot more likely to be motivated to read to the kids too.)

- If I can't keep the house clean, I don't really deserve to sit down for ten minutes and put my feet up. (Never mind that you're in a life phase of almost never sitting still due to chasing after a toddler, and that sitting down for ten minutes while they nap might make you a much kinder person the rest of the afternoon.)

- If I haven't hung out with the kids in the evening, I shouldn't ignore them so I can go take a bath. (Never mind that you can barely be civil with them right now because you're so frazzled from work, and taking a bath while they watch a cartoon might give you enough patience to have a good evening with them.)

All of these phrases are examples of using self-care as rewards and punishment. *If I do [this thing for others], then I am deserving of care. If I don't do [this thing for others], I am bad and will deny myself care.*

Self-care is not a reward, it's part of the process.

✏️ Field Notes: Ridiculously Simple Self-Care Rules

If our habit is to put off self-care until we've reached some elusive level of productivity, we can get so used to putting it off that we forget how to sense our needs at all. To avoid this, we're going to set a self-care parameter.

You're going to make yourself some ridiculously simple self-care rules. These are your nonnegotiable terms. These are the rules you follow because your logical self realizes that they matter, even if your emotional self is feeling guilty or says things like, "I don't have time."

Self-Care Rules

Make yourself three ridiculously simple self-care rules and stick to them. For instance, here are the rules I made for myself when my kids were one, four, and six. As you'll see, they were very basic. These rules helped me begin to realize I had to keep myself in the picture as well as the kids. By the way, they still work as the kids have gotten older. The rules were:

No. Don't wait. Go pee. You will perhaps appreciate the "go pee" commandment if you've ever been stuck under a *finally* sleeping baby with a full bladder and been forced to wake him or her to relieve yourself.

Make yourself lunch too. Why was I making three lunches and then grabbing myself crackers? This goes for other meals and snack time too.

For goodness' sake, go to sleep. Go to sleep. Is this as tough for you as it has been for me? The house is so quiet. No matter how exhausted I am, I'm tempted to stay up just a bit longer. The problem is that the next day I'm foggy-headed, quicker to anger, and less motivated to get things done like, oh, the laundry, for instance.

Whatever stage you're at in parenting—whether tots or teens— make yourself three ridiculously simple rules for self-care. Write them down in your day planner, on a sticky note by your desk, or as a note on your phone. Use these three simple rules to start making self-care part of the process.

EXAMPLES OF RULES YOU COULD MAKE FOR YOURSELF

- I bring a water bottle with me every day.
- If I'm feeling foggy, tired, or confused, I start with REST.
- I always eat lunch. No exceptions.
- I start my day by drinking a glass of water.
- Don't say yes unless it's a *heck yeah!* yes.
- Breakfast. Every day. For real.
- Stand up and stretch every half hour.
- After work I get to take ten minutes alone before talking to kids.
- We don't do more than three stops for errands in a day.
- Kids have to ask before coming into my bedroom.
- I never loan out my e-reader so that I always have something to read.
- The sparkling water is only for Mama.

These are just ideas—what do you need to remind yourself of on a daily basis? Choose three things.

MY RIDICULOUSLY SIMPLE SELF-CARE RULES

....

....

....

....

....

....

....

....

....

....

....

....

....

....

....

....

....

....

....

....

Mission: Speak to Yourself like Someone You Love

Beyond the physical self-care of getting enough sleep and nourishment, you also need to tend to mental and emotional self-care. This involves changing your internal dialogue. If your internal conversation is filled with comparisons and nasty comments about yourself, how can you expect to show your children how to love themselves?

This takes time to notice and change—but that's why we started earlier in the book learning about a growth mindset. We can grow our ability to be compassionate to ourselves.

Some of the top ways we disparage ourselves include: comparing ourselves to others, flinging hate at the way we look, and berating ourselves for mistakes. Let's see if we can begin to change some of those internal dialogues to be more empowering.

✔ Your Assignment: Talk to Your Four-Year-Old Self

It is up to you to take care of yourself.

Do you have a photo of yourself as a child? Get it out and take a look at that little one. Doesn't she or he deserve your care and love?

That four-year-old is still with you, and you are the only person who knows just what he or she needs. It is up to you to take care of yourself. For many of us, it is surprisingly uncomfortable. You deserve care. And *you* are the person who must care for yourself.

Stop your mean internal monologues. You do not deserve to be berated by anyone, including yourself. When you can give yourself loving kindness, you can refill your reserves, heal your emptiness, and continue caring for others.

Put up a photo of yourself as a child somewhere you will see it often. The next time you realize you're berating yourself, think about that young child. Would you talk to her that way? Would she learn anything from her mistakes if you called her stupid or worthless? How could you speak more gently to yourself? To care for your family, perhaps you can start by discovering how to speak kindly to yourself.

Mission: Learning to Trust Yourself

It takes a certain amount of trust in yourself to move toward a mindset of including self-care as part of the process.

You have to learn to trust that taking care of yourself is a healthy part of being interdependent. You don't have to live in the extremes of either totally indulging yourself and ignoring others or totally caring for others and ignoring yourself. In between, there is a healthy space that acknowledges that at some points in time as parents, we've got to come first, and at some points our children's needs must come first.

In order to keep yourself from swinging wildly on that pendulum between caring for yourself and caring for others, it's essential to develop trust in yourself.

✔️ Your Assignment: Follow Your Joy

Start with a small step of trusting yourself. Your assignment is to follow your joy. Today choose something you like. Whether it's the coffee mug you prefer, the place you sit at lunch, or the music you want to listen to.

This simple exercise was an eye-opener for me. I am the main grocery shopper at my house, and one day I decided that when I'm at the store, I can choose a yogurt flavor I like. I was surprised how far my own tastes had become submerged in those of my family.

Vanilla yogurt—I don't get that flavor; nobody likes it . . . oh, except me.

Today, try choosing something for yourself.

🕵️ Mission: Find Unexpected Downtime

After getting used to the idea that we have to take care of ourselves in the most basic ways, finding unexpected opportunities for downtime is the next achievement to unlock. Again, for constant caregivers, these opportunities may show up and then quickly be dismissed due to guilt. However, I had a moment that changed how I saw these unexpected moments of rest.

Tugged in Two Directions

One day in the spring, my three kids were out back hiding plastic eggs for each other. I was in my bedroom, which faces the backyard, and I'd catch glimpses of them as they played their game. I was just folding some clothes, but I was totally content in my room, happy to have quiet for a few moments, happy that they were getting along so well and I could have peace to finish a task. Then I heard them laughing, and the peaceful feeling, instead of increasing, began to evaporate. I felt guilty that I wasn't out there and yet tugged in two directions because I was really needing time to myself.

One of my sons came in with a huge grin on his face a few minutes later. "Mama! We've been playing Easter Bunny!" He breathlessly described their game to me and then, satisfied he'd updated me on the fun they were having, ran off. "Okay, I have to go! It's my turn to be the bunny next!" and with that I realized something very important.

I don't always need to be involved for their happiness to count.

Of course, my presence is important in their lives, but I am not their only connection to the world. In this instance, my kids were building sibling bonds and making happy memories together, and doing a fine job of it without my assistance.

My children have other relationships they need to develop, other experiences, other aspects of their lives besides me, and these can be very fulfilling and enjoyable for them. It is perfectly okay for me to allow that to happen, and to enjoy the stillness every once in a while, when I have the opportunity.

It is an art to know how to set aside a task and join kids in their play, and it is also an art to relax in the moment when they are happy and you are happy and you are not together.

You need both—your connection with your children, and your ability to let go and enjoy that they can be happy and explore their world without you.

✔️ Your Assignment: Allow Yourself to Observe from a Distance

Today give yourself permission to listen from another room, or observe from a distance and enjoy your child without guilt, and without thinking that you should be involved. You're attuned, and you will know when it's time to step back in.

📝 Field Notes: Bite-Sized Self-Care

It can be difficult, when you're busy with young kids, to take advantage of unexpected downtime, but we can make it easier to nurture ourselves during these short bits of breathing room throughout the day.

One of the biggest myths that keeps us from ever having time to ourselves is the notion that it requires long periods of time in order to be satisfying. So instead of being proactive in how we nurture ourselves, we don't plan, and we continue to feel run-down.

The pattern I've noticed:

- I get a few minutes of downtime that is unplanned for.
- I know I should be "productive" and I have a million things that should be done.

- The million things feel overwhelming, so I go online and check email or Facebook "real quick" instead.
- I zone out until life moves along and I have to move along too. I don't feel refreshed or more focused, and instead might feel guilty (about wasting time) or I might feel down or inadequate (if I spent time comparing my life to other people's on social media).

Sound familiar?

How could you use those few minutes of downtime in a way that does refresh and give energy instead of moving along in a fog of overwhelm?

The solution is to have a few simple, restful, replenishing activities at hand. This just takes a little forethought and believing that it's worth it to spend those few minutes on yourself.

I know, I *know*—you have a million things you should be doing. But really, you're not likely to get more than five, maybe ten minutes of peace anyhow, right? Might it be worthwhile to take ten minutes to yourself?

Take the time so your brain can stop spinning so fast, so that you can continue on in your day feeling a little more whole, and so that your kids can see an example of a person who takes care of themselves (as well as caring for everyone else).

Bite-Sized Self-Care List

Find a few things that nurture your soul that you can do even in busy times. These are little things you can do for yourself anytime—and they're especially good to do on days when you feel down.

Ideas for Bite-Sized Self-Care

- Reading a few pages of the novel you've been meaning to finish
- Making yourself a cup of coffee or tea
- Stepping outside for a breath of fresh air
- Turning on music you love
- Calling a friend
- Eating a healthy snack
- Putting on lotion

Bite-sized self-care activities are not giant change-the-world activities and instead are meant to remind you to be gentle with yourself and make self-care part of your day. What are the small actions that tell you that you are loved and you are valuable?

- List five things that make you feel nurtured that you can do in short amounts of time.

....

....

....

....

....

- Choose one way you'll connect with yourself in the coming week when you get a few minutes of downtime. How will you make sure this happens?

Examples:
- Reading (I will check a book out on my e-reader.)
- Crochet (I will put the project and instructions in a basket in the living room.)
- Drawing (I will find a pen I like and put that and a notebook out on my desk.)

What I will do:

....

....

....

How I will prepare:

....

....

....

Mission: Time to Yourself

Downtime Is Essential for Everyone—Including You

When was the last time you sat in a quiet room? After having no time to yourself, the simple space of not being needed or called upon can feel like you're quenching a thirst.

When I don't get time to myself, my brain starts to feel like it's short-circuiting—I can't think clearly, I get short-tempered, and I'm poor company.

Have you been through times like this? Or maybe you're there now. In case you're in that place right now:

- You're not crazy, selfish, overly needy, or broken for wanting uninterrupted time to yourself. Constant interruption is extremely stressful and really does compromise your ability to function. Everyone needs and deserves downtime—especially when parenting gets tough.

  It's hard to explain how extremely intense some phases of parenting can be, and whether you're being a caretaker during a family crisis, or whether this busy time is simply due to an intensive phase such as having infants or young children, it takes more of you than you may even realize.

- Look for your next opportunity to get that time alone, and don't feel guilty for taking it. You may have to inconvenience people to get time to yourself. Others expect your care all the time and may try to make you feel bad for needing a break, but you *do* need that mental break. Don't make it even harder on yourself by feeling guilty if you *do* get a time (or make a time) to take one.

- In the meantime, remind yourself to take care of the very basics of self-care: REST.

✅ Your Assignment: Time Grab

Beyond the unexpected moments, sometimes we need to make this downtime happen for ourselves.

One of the hardest parts about needing time to yourself is that as you become more exhausted, it's harder to push back against everyone needing you. This is your reminder that it is not likely anyone will give you permission to take care of you. You've got to grab that time, whether or not someone is offering it to you.

One Bounceback Parent told me, "I did kind of an immersion therapy approach! I would take a bath and force myself to stay in the tub and not run out to help my husband solve the problem. It might seem ridiculous . . . but I knew I wouldn't run down the hall dripping wet, covered in soap!"

Your assignment is to take one step toward having a chunk of time to yourself.

- You could call a friend and ask who she uses for a babysitter.
- Ask to swap a couple of hours of babysitting with a neighbor.
- Take a class at a gym or community center where they offer childcare.

Just make one step toward grabbing that time to yourself.

✅ Bonus Assignment: Turn Guilt into Gratitude

Do you have a chance to leave your child with a loving caregiver and take a break? Hooray! While you're away—your assignment is to turn guilt into gratitude. If you notice yourself feeling guilty for being away, experiment with what it feels like to say, "I'm so grateful that my child gets to experience loving relationships with other people," or "I'm grateful to get a chance to care for myself so that I can return refreshed."

Debriefing

Congratulations! Our infiltration into the Should Mama network has resulted in all Bounceback Parents being able to grow their practice of self-care. This has severely weakened the Should Mama and her nefarious henchmen Guilt and Perfection.

- You're clear that self-care means identifying your own needs mentally, emotionally, and physically and taking steps to meet those needs.
- You learned that you can feel guilty about doing self-care and do it anyway. One way to remember to push through that guilt is to think about all the reasons you have to take care of yourself.
- We began changing beliefs that keep you from taking care of yourself, including:
  - Thinking we have to earn the right to take care of our own needs by caring for others or being "productive."
  - Waiting for someone else to give us permission to care for ourselves.
  - Believing we are broken or wrong for not being able to do everything on our own.
- You've studied the very basics of self-care, which are to HALT for REST—if you're hungry, angry, lonely, or tired, you need to rehydrate, eat, step (outside), talk (to someone) . . . and get rest!
- You've discovered that you can practice self-care by doing it in "bite-sized" pieces. As you build the habit of trusting yourself to know what you need, it gets easier to know when it's okay to put your needs first.

More to Explore

Self-care is one of the more difficult Bounceback Parenting skills we practice, so we have many questions you can use to spark further thought about it. Use any of the following questions to deepen your understanding of self-care.

SELF-CARE BELIEFS

- Say to yourself, "I deserve loving care." How does that sit with you? Do you feel like you deserve to be cared for?
- In what ways do you model self-care for your child? What are three ways you could show your child that being kind to yourself is important? Is there something you do that they can imitate; for instance, drinking a glass of water, going on a walk, or going to bed earlier when you're tired?

PHYSICALLY: HOW DO YOU CARE FOR YOUR BODY?

- What negative phrase do you say to yourself about your body? Can you think of a positive phrase to replace the negative one? Example: "I hate my ugly stretch marks!" replaced with "Thank you, belly, for holding my babies." Find phrases that help you eliminate negative self-talk.
- List five things your body does that are amazing. They can be as simple as "taking this breath right now."
- List five *simple* things you can do during your day that nurture your body. These should be things that can be part of your

regular routine, like eating breakfast or stepping outside for breaks.

- How are you sleeping? Can you think of one change you could make to get better sleep this week?

MENTALLY: YOUR BODY NEEDS NUTRIENTS, BUT SO DOES YOUR BRAIN.

- What makes you feel more alert and interested in life? You are healthiest when you live with a sense of purpose, creative expression, and inspiration. What ways can you nurture these aspects of your life?
- What social-media strings do you need to cut to create an online space that nurtures you?
- What do you read/watch/talk about that's just mental clutter? For example: reading about problems you do not have, responding to people who do not want help, watching things that stress you out instead of rejuvenating you. What can you do to reclaim this mental space?

EMOTIONALLY: HOW DO YOU TEND TO YOUR INNER NEEDS?

- Who can you call who makes you feel loved and cared for?
- If you have no one you feel able to talk to, how could you develop a friendship this year? Envision having a close confidant—how does that relationship feel? You trust them . . . they trust you. How do you treat them? What do you share with them?

- How is your spirit? Do you long for more connection with God/ the universe/nature? If so, what is one simple way you can invite a deeper spiritual connection into your life?

....

....

....

....

....

....

....

....

....

....

....

....

....

....

....

....

....

....

....

....

....

....

....

....

....

....

....

....

....

....

....

....

....

....

....

CHAPTER FIVE

Operation Pumpkin Seed

Message from Ops

Notice! Maintenance required! Our emergency alert system has been malfunctioning. While this alert system is in place to give parents warning so they can protect their children from danger, it appears that the Should Mama in her anxiety has jammed the system in hyperresponse. The system has been going off at the slightest whiff of risk or struggle, causing parents everywhere to try to take control in situations where it would actually be more helpful to let children have room to grow.

To reset the system to a more tolerable and useful level, we're assigning you Operation Pumpkin Seed. This mission will help you allow for growth while also giving you the tools to calm anxiety.

- We'll explore why your emergency alert system goes off in the first place and why you try to take control.

- You will discover new levels of trust and build a strength-based perspective as you look at your children's strengths. They can build on these "islands of competence."
- You will be given the Bounceback Parenting League's secret of seventeen seconds for calming your own fears and giving your kids time to practice problem solving.
- You'll learn one question to ask before helping kids.
- And you'll calm the anxiety about making mistakes by making a plan for when they happen—ensuring you and your kids can all be lifelong learners.

Stop Squeezing Pumpkin Seeds

One day a couple of summers ago, my husband was taking the kids on a bike ride—the two boys on their bikes and our daughter in her trailer behind my husband's bike. I was staying home for some much-needed time to myself.

I bustled around them, being sure everyone had water, helping buckle helmets, sunscreening little noses, and checking if they had snacks. As they started to pull out of the yard I saw my daughter's bike trailer shade was up and I called out, "Wait, Azalea, do you want your shade down?"

My husband snapped, exasperated, "Liss, stop asking questions; she's fine! You ask them too many questions! We're fine and we just need to go!"

I waved them goodbye and felt a little indignant about his comment. (I was just trying to help!) But as I thought about it, I realized where he was coming from. Those questions were my way of making it a "perfect" outing. It was very hard for me to let things be out of my control and I constantly wanted to fix everything for everyone. Not only did it confuse my kids (*The sunshade? I'm about to go on a bike ride with Papa, now I need to think if there is a right answer to Mama about my sunshade?*), it also meant I was poor at letting other people be in charge, taking care of the kids—and doing all the caretaking on my own was exhausting me.

I had to look for the places I could let it be easy and spend less time fussing, trying to control and orchestrate and make things happen in a certain way.

I talked to my husband about it later and he gave me a great analogy. He said he continues to find with our family that sometimes it's important not to overthink things—to just go and do, to let things happen and to let people be. He said, "It's like trying to pinch a pumpkin seed—the tighter you squeeze, the harder it is to hold on to."

Have you ever shot a wet pumpkin or watermelon seed away from yourself by pinching it between your fingers? What would it be like to hold that pumpkin seed between your fingers?

You wouldn't exert too much pressure, because it would shoot away from you.

Likewise, you wouldn't let go completely, because, of course, then it would fall to the ground.

The amount of control we exert in our families is similar.

If we hold too tight, our family members become reliant on us to take care of everything, fearful of trusting themselves to make decisions, and resentful of us because of their lack of freedom.

If we let go completely, we lose the values and family rhythms that mean the most to us. We can provide a foundation—a framework to live within—yet also give room to grow.

Why do we hold on to control?

In my story about the bike ride, I was anxious. No, the anxiety wasn't logical—of course my husband could competently take the kids on a bike ride—but my Should Mama piped up, thinking of all the things he should do and wanting to get everything perfect. The Should Mama in me was anxious about the kids being uncomfortable, anxious about them riding their bikes, anxious about not being out there with them. Rather than feel these uncomfortable emotions, I tried to compensate with control. If I could control all the factors, from snacks to sunscreen, maybe it would calm that yucky anxious feeling.

Bounceback Parent Michelle explains this need for control quite well:

> I think for a lot of us (definitely me!) when we're feeling powerless and fearful, we tend to try to control our kids and the situation. When we are uncomfortable with emotions, instead of feeling them and looking inside ourselves and what they bring up for us, we try to control our kids and their emotions/behaviors that are triggering us.

If we want to allow people room to grow, we have to give up trying to control their every move and learn to manage our own emotions.

A few concepts have really helped me calm my urge to control my kids: learning about the growth mindset (as we talked about in chapter two), learning about having a strength-based perspective, and learning about encouraging resilience (the latter two we'll talk about in this chapter).

When we see our kids as people with positive intent who sometimes make mistakes, it's easier to calm our anxiety and become their guide and teacher rather than trying to take control.

Field Notes: Control

- What situations are most likely to make you want to take control? How does the sensation of wanting to take control feel in your body?

....

....

....

....

....

....

....

....

....

....

....

....

....

....

....

....

....

....

- What messages do you tell yourself that increase the urge to take control? What messages (from yourself or others) allow you to step back from control?

....

....

....

....

....

....

....

....

....

....

....

....

....

....

....

....

....

....

....

A Strength-Based Perspective

The Should Mama is fearful, fixated on what's going wrong. She forgets what's going right and definitely forgets about our most powerful tools—our strengths, or as Robert Brooks and Sam Goldstein put it in *Nurturing Resilience in Our Children*, our "islands of competence":

> *We must find each child's island of competence, since it is through our strength and abilities that we find joy, pleasure, and success in life.*

I love the visual of seeking out these islands. It creates a strength-based perspective from which we look for ways people are *capable* rather than ways they are lacking.

When you're trying to find a solution to a challenge in your family, any solution that builds on people's strengths, rather than focusing on why they are weak, is more likely to work. Our strengths give us a solid foundation to build on.

> Our strengths give us a solid foundation to build on.

Field Notes: Discovering Your Child's Strengths

It's easier to trust our kids to keep growing toward their best selves when we look for their strengths. You can encourage those strengths and use them as a foundation for building up areas where your child needs help.

Use these questions to uncover your child's strengths.

- Watch your kids play—what do they enjoy? What roles do they take on when they pretend? How do they interact with friends during play?

....

....

- What's something quirky about your child?

....

....

- What books or films does your child gravitate toward?

....

....

- What activities or subjects hold your child's attention?

....

....

- What does he or she do that makes you laugh?

....

....

- What does your child do that is outside of your comfort zone?

....

....

- What does he or she do regularly that frustrates or worries you?

....

....

Take a look at your answers to these questions. Do they point you toward any particular strengths? For instance:

- If your daughter declares her goal is to be a nature princess, collects leaves, watches bugs, and creates dirt "potions," does this point to a scientific curiosity about the natural world? A sense of adventure and beauty?
- If your son reads avidly about soldiers and battle, leads the kids in marching around the playground, and keeps his Lego tanks arranged perfectly on his bedroom shelf, does this point to a bent toward leadership and a love of order?
- If your daughter wears you down with her nonstop movement, talking at the top of her lungs, and running and jumping wherever she goes, does this mean she is also capable of inspiring others with her enthusiasm and using her energy for jobs that require physical strengths, like outdoor guiding?
- If your son worries you with his seeming oversensitivity to others' moods and his unwillingness to be flexible, is he also an understanding caretaker for young children and a great scorekeeper for family game night?

What strengths can you see in each of your kids? Write down a few for each child below.

....

....

....

....

....

....

....

....

....

....

....

....

....

....

....

....

....

....

....

....

....

Field Notes: Letting Your Child's Strengths Shine

The needs inventory in chapter three includes the question, "What activities or family jobs allow this child's unique skills to shine?" Now that you have a deeper knowledge of his or her strengths, you can expand on these ideas.

Build on Strengths

For each of your child's strengths, brainstorm a few ways this strength can be encouraged in your family. For instance:

You may have a son who is sensitive and likes to be in control, craving order and clear expectations. It may be very frustrating when he tries to tell everyone what to do. When you look at these attributes from a strength-based perspective you may see a person who is *sensitive and loving*, has a *strong appreciation of beauty and order*, and has *perseverance*.

Some ways to build on these strengths are:

- **Expression of love:** taking care of pets, writing thank-you notes, helping entertain a friend's baby, asking him about ways you can communicate better to increase the feeling of love in your family
- **Appreciation of beauty and order:** creating order in manageable spots like a drawer, shelf, or cupboard; picking a bouquet for the table; getting his opinion about how things look, such as a furniture arrangement or an art project
- **Perseverance:** giving him physical tasks like weeding or snow shoveling, asking him to be in charge of motivating the family through a task like cleaning the kitchen, helping him set goals and giving him tracking tools like a chart to fill in so he knows how he is doing on them

Can you do this for your own kids? The process of looking for their strengths and thinking about how they can use those strengths is extremely helpful for seeing your kids in a more positive light.

Noticing your children's (and partner's) strengths also helps you realize you are not alone. When you notice that your family members have their own strengths, it's easier to loosen control and find ways they can hold some of the responsibilities in the family instead of trying to do it all yourself.

Three of my child's strengths are:

....

....

....

Activities that build on these strengths are:

....

....

....

Mission: Seventeen Seconds to Reduce Anxiety

If we want to stop the emergency alert system from constantly going off in our heads, we need to be able to sit with some uncomfortable emotions. It's tempting to jump in to try to fix a situation or take control, especially if you're feeling anxious.

It's normal to feel that anxiety; that's okay. Much like the guilt we might feel during self-care, though: just because we feel it doesn't mean we need to act on it. We want to allow others room to grow, but they don't get the chance if we never give them time.

I accidentally discovered a simple but effective way to disengage my emergency alert system. I was reading about communication and interruption when I found this simple method. You can use the seventeen-second rule as a gentle way to restrain yourself from immediately jumping in.

The Difference of Seventeen Seconds

"Are you ever going to let me finish a sentence?!"

"Mom! I can do it myself!"

Why were the people I love getting mad at me? I was just trying to help, and hey, I'm not interrupting, I just thought they were done talking!

I really didn't want to admit I was an interrupter. Then I read in *The 5 Love Languages: The Secret to Love That Lasts* that the average person doesn't go more than seventeen seconds before interrupting the person talking.

Seventeen measly seconds? Really? I certainly wasn't that bad. . . .

I decided to find out. I started by trying out waiting seventeen seconds during conversations with my husband and my kids, counting silently to seventeen before speaking my thoughts . . . and oh dear. I was shocked at how often I was ready to interrupt during that first seven seconds, let alone seventeen seconds. I discovered that frequently when I think one of my family members is done talking, he or she is actually just taking a breath or needing time to think before answering.

Encouraged by how powerful this pause was in conversations, I began to use seventeen seconds as a waiting time when I saw one of my kids struggle. Resisting the urge to jump in to fix something or give a suggestion, I waited. How could it be that in only seventeen seconds so much could happen?

The Beauty of a Noninterruption

One day we were sitting together as my kids worked on some intricate Lego structures and one of my sons got really frustrated about a mistake.

My brain desperately wanted me to say, "Would you like some help?"

But I remembered my seventeen-seconds plan and my mouth was quiet. One. Two. Three. Four. . . .

He started to get more loud and frustrated about his task, but he kept at it.

I kept counting. Eight. Nine. Ten. . . .

My urge to rescue him was calming down as I realized my child needed this time to struggle with difficulties and to problem-solve.

Fourteen. Fifteen. Sixteen. . . .

"Mama—I think I can change this. I thought this was totally messed up, but I found a solution!"

Oh. *Wow.* If I had started in with a suggestion a few seconds earlier it would have robbed him of that moment!

Yup—seventeen seconds makes a big difference.

I am not completely "cured" of interrupting, but seventeen seconds is giving the people around me a chance to talk, and it's giving me a chance not only to hear them but to let them show me how capable they really are—letting those strengths shine.

> Seventeen seconds makes a big difference.

✅ Your Assignment: Wait Seventeen Seconds

- When your child is facing a difficulty and you're tempted to jump in and save them, *wait*. Give them time to work through the frustration and build resilience. Allow them the possibility of their own victory.
- When you've asked a question and gotten no response, or a short "I don't know," *wait*. See if a few more seconds of silence on your part will allow your child time to think and answer more fully.
- When you think of something important you want to add to the conversation, *wait*. Hang on a few more moments and see if the person you're talking with has finished their thought.

🕵 Mission: Increase Problem-Solving Skills

I came into parenting with a mindset of wanting to make my kids happy. I equated a peaceful home with successful motherhood, and this means I have often offered help in the name of keeping the situation calm, instead of allowing my kids to face frustration and experience finding their own solution.

While I still highly value peace, I am coming to terms with the fact that in order to learn how to deal with the problems my kids will undoubtedly face, they must get lots and lots and *lots* of practice problem solving. That's why I have been asking myself one question each time I am tempted to help my kids, or when they ask me for help: Is this something my child can do by themselves?

We can help kids develop problem-solving skills and resilience by allowing them to experience their own successes instead of taking over and doing things for them that they could do on their own. As Brooks and Goldstein point out in *Nurturing Resilience in Our Children*:

> *The more successes a child experiences, the more likely that child will develop a resilient mindset. However, there are qualifications to that statement. Two major factors that determine whether a child's successes nurture a resilient mindset are (a) whether the child believes the successes are based, at least in part, on his or her own resources and efforts, and (b) whether the successes are judged to be important to the child and significant others (friends, family).*

✔️ Your Assignment: Hone Your Helping Instincts

The next time your child faces a challenge and you're tempted to jump in to solve it for them, ask yourself: Is this something my child can do by themselves? If the answer is yes—you think your child can do this task on their own—hone your helping instincts with these considerations:

- **Is this a good chance to allow them, or push them, to do the work themselves?** Sometimes it's possible to push a bit. And sometimes, even if we are capable of a task, we need help, particularly if we're hungry, angry, lonely, or tired. (See? We can use the HALT acronym here too!)
- **Is this an opportunity when it's possible to let them take their time to practice a daily life skill?** With younger children, we often jump in without even being asked, simply because it takes

a long time for kids to do things themselves. The more independent they get, the easier things will be for you both.

- **Am I feeling uncomfortable seeing my child struggle?** Using the seventeen-second rule has been very helpful for me in breaking the habit of seeing every struggle as an emergency from which to rescue my child. That short wait helps me retrain my brain so that my internal panicked Should Mama learns that I can handle feeling uncomfortable for a few moments and it's not an emergency.

- **Is this a new task that's causing my child to feel unsure or overwhelmed?** When we're learning something new, we all need lots of encouragement and time for training. Many of the tasks we think should be easy are still new to our kids, or even when they're not new, our kids are growing and learning so much each day that the old sometimes still feels new.

- **Can I get my child thinking about the solution themselves?** When my kids ask me things that I believe they can do or find out on their own, I might ask a guiding question like, "Where would you find that information?" Or when they're overwhelmed, instead of saving them from frustration I might say, "You seem a bit overwhelmed by this task. What is the next little step you can take?"

If you ask yourself whether this is something your child can do on their own and the answer is no, this is not something you believe your child can do, my next question would be: Is this something I can support them in doing at least partly by themselves?

- Your three-year-old wants to make lunch. If she can't spread the peanut butter, can she work with you and plop the jam on the bread? Could she press the pieces together?
- Your five-year-old wants to do his own laundry. He might not know yet how to do the entire laundry task, but can he bring his clothes to the washing machine? Can he pour in the soap?
- Your twelve-year-old wants help applying to a new school. You may need to sign the papers, but can he fill out the information on them? He may need help with how to request a copy of his report card, or phrasing a polite request for a reference letter, but can he send the email himself?

All of the little actions we do so easily as adults are built out of thousands and thousands of practice times doing those actions. We have a large "bank" of ready actions for facing a new problem or frustration. We can add to our kids' bank of solutions.

Each time we support our child through doing something on their own, we help them build resilience and increase their own competence. I often struggle with how much longer this takes, but I am reminding myself that when I shortcut by doing something for my kids that they could manage on their own, it's not really a shortcut. It only leaves something they will need to practice later.

My job is to raise capable, independent people. I better give them lots of chances to practice, mess up, and try again while the stakes are not as high as they will be once they're out on their own.

Mission: Plan for Mistakes

Mistakes become less threatening as you experience being able to learn from them and make new choices for the future. You'll also discover you can guide your children in becoming better at assessing risks and learning from their own mistakes. It all starts with a simple plan.

Our Opportunity to Get Creative

When I was twelve, I went to my mom frustrated and near tears. My drawing wasn't turning out how I wanted and I felt like ripping it to pieces. "Well, Liss," she said, smiling, "this is our opportunity to really get creative!" Her attitude was so positive, so assured that now we could simply rework whatever I was drawing.

We played out this scenario over and over again. Her enthusiasm for creatively managing mistakes gave us kids permission to experiment, to try new things and risk failing. When it came to art, she showed us that we could look at mistakes not as a roadblock but as an exciting challenge that might even make our art better than we expected. She says, "When you make a mistake, first you say, 'Oh no!' Then you say, 'Now what?' And finally, 'What if . . . ?'"

Not all mistakes are so simple to grow from, but my mom's positive handling of mistakes gave my siblings and me a helpful lens to look at mistakes through. When I began to apply this thinking to more of my life, I realized that mistakes are inevitable. It's easier and more satisfying to spend my energy learning from mistakes rather than trying to avoid making them in the first place.

Parenting with a growth mindset means you see mistakes as opportunities to learn. This is easier if we have a plan for mistakes—our own and our kids'.

Plan for mistakes by deciding what you will do to learn from them. Ask these questions after a mistake:

- **What happened?** Try to be as nonjudgmental as possible. "Just the facts," so you can understand better why things happened the way they did. This is not a time for criticism and blame.
- **Why do you think it happened?** Again, try to stick with a non-shaming assessment of why things went wrong. The point is to be able to learn from this, not to punish someone.
- **What will you do in the future? What did you learn from this setback?** This is where the reflection and learning come together. Visualize how you can apply this lesson to your life in the future. If you are asking these questions with your child, let them come up with what they'll do in the future. It may take practice to be able to answer this question, for kids and for adults, but the more we practice, the better we get at being able to learn from mistakes and see the way forward.

✅ Your Assignment: Find a Great Mistake

Your son forgets to do his homework; your daughter spills the milk when getting a bowl of cereal, or breaks a dish when trying to take it from the cupboard. Try the three mistake questions with your child. Can you guide them gently through assessing their mistake and learning from it?

Beyond that, the next time you make a mistake, go through these questions for yourself and see if you can find your way forward.

When we trust that we're all capable of learning and that learning comes from making mistakes and readjustments, we can encourage growth.

Field Notes: Building Skills, Handling Mistakes

- What skills can you teach your children and allow them to practice? (For instance, how to make their own lunch for school, how to cut with a knife, how to introduce themselves or order their own meals at a restaurant.)

....

....

....

....

- How can you react positively when your child "messes up" or makes a mistake? (For instance, a plate gets dropped when they're setting the table or they spill the juice when pouring it. What do they need to learn for next time?) Write your own example of a mistake and what you could say.

....

....

....

....

....

....

....

....

Debriefing

The Should Mama keeps us in her grip, setting off our emergency alert system because she fears mistakes. She keeps track of all the things we should do to avoid them. She isn't really mean; she's just scared.

Our desire to control stems from fear of getting it wrong, and the mistaken belief that control equals safety, security, and certainty. We try to protect those we love from harm, but our real job is to help them handle the challenges that will come their way in the future.

- When we try to control everything, it increases our stress and exhaustion, reduces our ability to enjoy our families, and restricts growth.
- One way to think about control is to picture what happens when you pinch a slippery pumpkin seed—it's very hard to hold on to. The harder you press, the more frustrating it becomes.
- We try to control things out of fear. It's easier to allow for growth if we remember that challenges help our kids build resilience.
- We can try proactive coaching with our children—teaching them how to do something instead of banning them from it.

- ◆ We can help our children to develop their own resilience and problem-solving skills by using the seventeen-second rule.
- ◆ We can expand our ability to sit with uncomfortable emotions—realizing that these are opportunities for connection just as the joyful emotions are.
- ▪ We can plan for mistakes, knowing that assessing our mistakes provides opportunity for creativity and learning.

More to Explore

- ▪ If we feel overwhelmed by all the things we want to control, no doubt our children feel that way sometimes too. Are there perhaps areas where we're asking them to be in control before they're ready for that responsibility? Are there areas where they have grown and are ready for more autonomy and control?
- ▪ What messages did you hear about being in control when you were a child?
- ▪ Journal about a time you were forced by outside circumstances to let go of something that you had tried hard to control. How did it go? How did it feel?
- ▪ Sometimes we let go of too much. Think about a time you completely let go and then found you needed more control again. What did you learn?
- ▪ Try staying with an unpleasant feeling or emotion for thirty seconds or so. The next time you're irritated, upset, or fearful, simply "be present" with that emotion. Don't judge it; just stop and *feel it* for a moment. What is that experience like?

CHAPTER SIX

Operation Permission to Pause

MESSAGE FROM OPS

I am pleased to welcome you to one final training mission. Your mission, should you choose to accept it, will pit you against the Should Mama's diabolical team of henchmen: Comparison, Distraction, Ordinary Chaos, Perfection, and Guilt. You've been working on creating a growth mindset while connecting and being more kind to yourself. You are open to possibilities and growth. Giving yourself permission to pause may be your greatest challenge, and I believe you're ready for it. Here's how we'll defeat the Should Mama's henchmen.

- First, we'll pause to work on clarifying your values and purpose—your big picture. When you take the time to really get to know yourself and your own values, you are more able to relax and know where you can be flexible and where you are not willing to bend. You are less likely to get distracted comparing yourself to others, because you realize we each have our own priorities, and yours may be different from someone else's.

- You'll then improve your growth mindset by pausing for a weekly check-in to ask yourself if you're practicing your values in your daily life. You'll be able to notice what you're doing well and where you want to grow.
- Then, to further increase the alignment of your daily life with your big-picture goals and values, you'll practice celebrating the small victories and sweet moments of life that no one else gives you permission to pause for.

Be a Real Hero

When we read stories about heroes, they're usually the people rescuing someone from a burning building or saving the day with acts of bravery and daring. And that does fit the definition of hero: a person noted for courageous acts or nobility of character.

What about when those acts of courage are quieter? Less flashy? Sometimes the heroes in our own stories are like that, yet they are nonetheless heroic.

My husband and I were talking about some of the ambitious young staff members at our business (we own a brewery), and my husband said of one of them, "He never stops; it's always emergency mode for him because I think he likes being a hero. . . . He doesn't realize yet that almost nothing is so important that it won't wait overnight, and the real hero is the guy who comes home for dinner."

My husband used to be that guy—never home, the hero at work

but not for his family. The evening that this conversation took place he'd had a crazy day, and I'd already figured he wouldn't be home for dinner, so when he walked in at six thirty I felt very cared for. His action of coming home made me feel that the kids and I are a priority to him.

Heroes are brave, selfless, and there when you need them.

- When we want closeness and connection for our family, being a hero means showing up.
- When we want clear communication, it is an act of bravery to be vulnerable and share something about yourself, or listen as a family member shares with you.
- When we want to be more present, being a hero means we courageously let go of what doesn't matter so much to be there for what does. It means having the courage to say no.

Being a hero is having the courage to be who you are and the perseverance to keep on improving yourself, rather than comparing yourself or your family to other people or families. You can only be this hero if you take some time to clarify what really matters to you.

Field Notes: Get Your Bearings

When you're out on a hike, it makes sense to pause every so often to get your bearings, making sure you know where you are and where you're headed. We can apply this to family life as well by pausing to reorient ourselves to what matters most. When you know your core values, it's easier to make choices about what you say yes to and what you pass on. It's easier to be a hero to your family when you have clarified what matters most to you. Your core values give you direction and reduce guilt about choosing to tend to what's essential.

- **If you had only a handful of concepts with which to lead your family, what would they be?** It's a big question, but the good news is you don't have to come up with the perfect answer right now. Start thinking about it and it'll become clearer over time. What are the values that come to mind as being the foundation of your family? List your family's top five to eight values. Take a look at the following words for ideas:

    courage, love, kindness, bravery, faith, determination, persistence, positive attitude, gratitude, hospitality, forgiveness, grace, generosity, friendship, family, exploration, confidence, truthfulness, listening, fun, compassion, friendliness, thoughtfulness, patience, understanding, learning, optimism, humor, playfulness, respect, kindness, curiosity, creativity . . .

    Our family's top values are:

    ....

    ....

    ....

    ....

    ....

    ....

    ....

    ....

- **List five or more words describing the feeling of the relation-ship you want with your kids.** Examples of words you might use include: *close, connected, respectful, playful* . . .

....

....

....

....

....

- **What matters to you in the big picture?** That your kids are *in-dependent and happy? Successful and fulfilled?* What do those things mean to you? Finish this sentence: "What really matters to me is . . ." (Use the note pages in the back of this book if you need more space to write.)

....

....

....

....

....

....

....

....

....

■ **I hope my children remember this about me:**

....

....

....

....

....

....

The Touchstones of Childhood

When I was a kid, my dad lived an hour away from me. He would pick up my brother and me every Friday after school and bring us back to our mom's on Sunday evening. Over the years we spent hours and hours in the car together.

His cars changed over time, but one thing didn't. Whether it was the drafty VW hatchback with a hole in the floor, the trusty white Saab with the beaded seat covers, or the secondhand silver minivan, these cars were a place for singing.

"Papa! We're learning songs about the United States in class. Let's sing 'America the Beautiful'!"

"Papa! Sing me that song about love and rainbows and the girl who dances!"

"Do you know the words to 'La Bamba'?"

"Papa! Turn up Simon and Garfunkel and let's sing along!"

We sang and sang.

I don't think he planned ahead for this singing to be a touchstone for me. Singing together was just something we all loved, but when my dad died at the age of forty-nine, my brother and I were thirteen and sixteen. We had a relatively short time with our dad, and those times singing together in the car are some of my most treasured memories. They are a touchstone from my childhood, giving me an unshakable certainty that I was loved.

We can't always choose what our children will remember.

We also have very little say over when we will leave this earth.

What we *can* do is show love while we can, even if it's while driving along in a beat-up old car.

✎ Field Notes: Making Memories

In the Get Your Bearings field notes (see page 141), you wrote down a few things you want your kids to remember about you. The Making Memories page takes that one step further. Let's take a look at those things you want your kids to remember, and think of something concrete in your daily life that will help create those memories. For instance, I wrote down that I want my kids to remember I smiled a lot. Actions I can take: smile when my child walks into a room.

What I want my kids to remember about me	What actions can I take to create these memories?
....	....
....	....
....	....

....

....

....

....

....

....

....

....

....

....

....

....

....

....

✏️ Field Notes: Weekly Check-in

We fend off the Should Mama's henchmen Confusion and Guilt and improve our growth mindset when we pause for a weekly check-in to see how we're living up to our stated values, what we're doing well, and where we want to grow.

Make a commitment to do a weekly check-in with yourself for the next few weeks. One of the hardest things about parenting is how unpredictable it can be—our best-laid plans get scrambled in moments. This makes it doubly important to look back and give ourselves credit for what we've accomplished, even if it wasn't what was planned. Otherwise, all our focus tends to be on the negative, keeping us in a cycle of feeling guilty and inadequate. Noticing the good helps us move upward, out of this cycle.

> **Noticing the good helps us move upward.**

Weekly Check-in Questions

Big-picture reminder: To refocus yourself on your larger purpose, jot down a sentence or even just a few words to remind yourself of your big picture for family life (e.g., feelings you want to nurture, activities you do together, core values).

What I did last week: Write down at least three positive things you did for your relationship with your child last week. Small things count. Give yourself credit for what's going well. Remember the growth mindset—we're always learning.

Major lesson: Write down something you learned last week about your child or yourself that you'd like to remember. What insights did you gather? How can you re-create or avoid this in the future?

One thing I will do this week: What one thing can you do this week to live like the person you want to be with your family? Yes, you'll probably do more than one, but what one thing will you commit to?

Visit our online headquarters for a printable weekly check-in page.

Mission: Pause to Celebrate

We daydream about the victories of our life, especially the big ones. In the movies, the film score is triumphant, soaring music. We look forward to our victories, thinking how exciting they'll be! Maybe we'll have a special dinner, dress up, decorate, and have a party. But how does it really play out?

Graduations and weddings tend to be well celebrated, but those are the big ones. When you think about the victories that happen in your day-to-day life—do you really notice them? Many of the events that make up the sparkle of now and the touchstones of our memories are in fact small moments. Do we slow down to acknowledge them in real time?

What the Should Mama doesn't want you to know is that no one gives you permission to slow down and notice these small victories, but by slowing down to celebrate anyway, we can create more joyful memories, and confirm and strengthen our family's sense of purpose.

The first time your child rides a bike with no training wheels; the day you finally open the doors to the new business; the first haircut for your toddler—all great. But what about the day your six-year-old loses her first tooth, gets a good grade on an assignment, or puts her toys away without prompting? Small victories.

In the moment, no bells ring to tell you to pause. The laundry doesn't fold itself, dinner still needs to get made, and the six-year-old—forget it, she's already on to another activity . . . and where did she go, anyway? The ordinary chaos will not take a break. Now might not be the time . . .

But *wait*! If you don't pause to celebrate these small victories, if this isn't an important moment, what really is? Don't these small victories make up the stuff of life that we *really* want to remember? They happen all the time, don't they? These little markers in our life that say, *You've done it! Hooray!* And if we don't slow down enough to celebrate them, no one will do it for us.

Ten Ways to Celebrate Small Victories with Kids

Here are ten ways to celebrate with kids that we have used in our family. Like our simple birthday traditions, these don't have to be complicated, just a way to help everyone notice the good stuff.

- Make a bunting or a banner to hang—this can be as simple as hanging some streamers.
- Have a tea party or a picnic.
- Make a meal that says, *We're celebrating!*
- Light a candle at dinner. Include talking about the small victories of your day in your family's dinnertime rituals.
- Ask your child to draw a picture to commemorate the victory and then display it proudly.

- Write the story down in a blank book and read it as part of bedtime.
- Give each child a small treasure to put in a memory box.
- Take a family drive together.
- Call Grammy and tell her about your small victory!
- Write a blog post about it—or scrapbook it, or share on Facebook or 23snaps (this is what we use for sharing family photos, as it's more private) and then call your kids over and show them so they can see that you're telling people how great they are!

✔️ Your Assignment: Celebrate!

Next time you notice a small victory in your family life, pause to celebrate. It can be as easy as giving high fives. Just notice and celebrate.

Debriefing

Congratulations! By giving yourself permission to pause, to focus on your purpose and values, you've gained clarity about what matters most to you. This clarity makes it much harder for the Should Mama to overwhelm you, as you can decide if her "should" matches your "big picture" of what you want to nurture in your family. In this operation, you've learned:

- We need to pause to reflect on what matters to us, to integrate what we've learned, to plan for what's to come, and to savor what has occurred. Nobody will give you permission to pause, so you have to give it to yourself.

- We need regular reflection in order to integrate what we're learning and see how we're growing every day. One way to pause to reflect is by journaling regularly.
- We can pause to celebrate small victories and thereby increase our family's sense of purpose and joy.

More to Explore

- If your family had a slogan, what do you think it would be?
- What actions do you need to take in order to give yourself permission to pause from time to time? What are you running from? What will happen if you stop?
- How can you be a hero to your children? For instance, taking them along on errands, playing a game with them, or helping them with a tough homework assignment. Remember, real heroes *show up*.
- What do you enjoy about your children right now?
- Have you ever sat with your children and helped them look back on their past week? What have they learned? What are they planning for the coming week?

....

....

....

....

....

....

....

....

....

....

....

....

....

....

....

....

....

....

....

....

....

....

....

....

....

....

Congratulations!

You are now a full Bounceback Parenting League agent!

- You've learned about parenting with a growth mindset. We're all works in progress, and we can all improve and grow starting from right where we are.
- You've learned about connection as a practice and have begun to recognize the small ways you can weave presence and acceptance into your everyday life.
- You've learned that self-care is part of the process and made steps to recognize and tend to your own needs as part of your daily routine.
- You're ready to empower others by seeing people's strengths, allowing for growth, and learning from mistakes together.
- And, finally, finding your purpose and reflecting on it regularly has prepared you to continue applying these principles to your life.

I am honored to serve alongside you.

Always learning,
Your director of ops,

Alissa Marquess

For a printable reminder of the principles of Bounceback Parenting, go to our online headquarters to download the Bounceback Parenting Credo.

CHAPTER SEVEN

Staying on Target

A s director of ops, I'm leaving you with a few more tools to help you stay on target. Some days you're simply exhausted. Some days you're angry, resentful, sad, lonely, or sick of parenting. When these emotions crop up, it's hard to remember the simple things that make for good days with your kids.

When your reserves are low, you can use the following tools—for getting through a rough patch, finding a boost of motivation, or discovering ideas for simple ways to reconnect. In short, they will help your day go more smoothly.

Parenting Reminder for the Hardest Days

 You are not alone in having some hard days. You can find a printable version of this reminder in our online headquarters.

PARENTING REMINDER

I don't have to be perfect.

It doesn't matter I'm not perfect.

Acknowledging my child's feelings and my own allows us to connect.

Downtime is critical for everyone.

I can start over from here.

I can talk to someone.

Six Easy Ways to Turn Around a Bad Day

I've had plenty of days when it feels like I've been snapping at my kids all day and have probably snuck more than my fair share of dark chocolate chips from the pantry while I desperately wished I could fast-forward to bedtime.

Strangely, chocolate doesn't fix everything, and I didn't want to spend so many days grumpy and then feeling guilty for yelling, so over time, with plenty of opportunities to practice them, I've developed my top strategies for turning around a bad day.

It's nothing magical, and some days I've had to use a pretend-nice voice while I fume silently to myself, but these strategies do usually work to shift the mood in my house. Soon I find I'm not having to pretend and I'm back to feeling connected to and appreciative of my children.

Try one of these strategies when you need to pull your day back on track. You can find a printable page of this list in our online headquarters.

Six Easy Ways to Turn Around a Bad Day

1. TAKE CARE OF BASIC NEEDS. Take care of yourself too. Comfortable people are far less grumpy.
   - Has everyone, including you, eaten some decent food recently?
   - Has everyone had enough water today?
   - Is anyone too cold or too hot? Maybe coming down with a cold or seasonal allergies?

2. GIVE TEN MINUTES OF FOCUSED ATTENTION. Filling kids' attention cups can help you get a break too.
   - Read together—grab a pile of books and read together on the couch until the pile is gone. Hold the grumpiest child on your lap or right next to you to increase their feeling of connection and calm.
   - Play a game—keep a variety of board games and card games around that are fun for everyone.
   - Color together—get out drawing supplies and tell a story about something that happened this week, listen to music, or put on an audiobook while everyone colors. Try working on a drawing together.

3. DO SOME SENSORY PLAY. Keep a list of quick sensory ideas so you always have an easy activity.
   - Play-Doh is a miracle worker—you might include plastic animals, beads, straws, or cookie cutters.

- Water play is soothing—include cups and a couple of drops of food color. Finger paint in the tub. Give a shower or a bath with lavender oil and calming music.
- Make a quick sensory bin—put cornmeal, oats, salt, or beans in a baking dish and let your kids swish their hands through; give them toy cars or spoons to play with in the sensory bin.

4. HEAD OUTSIDE. With the right clothing, you can go outside in every season.

- Go look for five signs of the season in your yard.
- Walk around the block—try to find a bird.
- Or just take out the garbage together—do something to change the scenery.

5. GET SILLY. Our kids live in their imaginations, so let this help you.

- Change a chore into a story—*"Oh my gosh!* I just realized the grouchy ghost came into our house! We've got to grab all these blocks and hide them from him or we'll all be grouchy! Fast!"
- Pretend to be ridiculously incompetent—putting underpants on your head instead of in the drawer, falling over, pretending you can't do a task—letting your child laugh and outshine you.
- Loudly and suddenly declare something silly—"Stop! It's time to . . . dance like a camel!" or "Talk like a pirate!" or "Tell your best joke!" or "See who can go cross-eyed and stick out their tongue."

6. TAKE A TIME-OUT. Sometimes we need to give ourselves a time-out to hit the reset button on our day.

- Call a friend—conversation with another adult can help you remember that you're not alone, and maybe it will give you an idea how to change the situation.

- Stop trying to fix the situation—make sure kids are in a safe spot, separated if need be, and retreat to another room. Ignore the screaming or pounding on the door unless someone is hurt. Breathe and plan your next move. You don't have to be a happy parent in order not to be a yelling parent.

You do not need to be perfect. Everyone has bad days; most of us have dealt with parenting rage and parenting guilt, but that doesn't make us bad parents, just lifelong learners—growing through our mistakes. When you notice something needs to change, you are empowered to make that change!

You do not need to be perfect.

Though no one can go back and make a brand-new start, anyone can start from now and make a brand-new ending.

—CARL BARD

Self-Care Checklist

Sometimes we're too overwhelmed, sad, scared, or simply too tired to know what it means to take care of ourselves. If you find yourself feeling this way, remember the mission HALT for REST in chapter four and use this list for guidance on what you can do right now to help yourself feel better. You can find a printable version in our online headquarters.

Am I too warm or too cold?

◆ If so, change clothing or the temperature of your surroundings.

Have I gotten sleep lately?

◆ If not, try taking a ten-minute nap if possible.

◆ If you can't sleep right now, be gentle on yourself as you make it through the day, and prioritize sleep as soon as possible.

Am I dehydrated?

◆ Drink a glass of water.

◆ If plain water doesn't appeal to you, try warm water with lemon, herbal tea, sparkling water, or water infused with fruit.

Have I eaten anything in the past four hours?

◆ Grab a snack that includes some protein, such as nuts and fruit, yogurt, or cheese and crackers.

Do I need to step outside? Stretch?

◆ Walk outside and let your eyes rest on the horizon. Take a deep breath and stretch your arms.

Do I need to talk to someone about my thoughts or feelings?

◆ Call a friend, reach out in a supportive online group, or write in your journal. (You can use prompts from this book!)

◆ Be patient with yourself if you are experiencing intense emotions such as grief, fear, or anger. If possible, take steps to reduce outside responsibilities when working through difficult emotions.

Have I had any time alone recently?

- Call a friend or babysitter to arrange for at least half an hour alone.
- Look for your next unexpected downtime.
- Use your bite-sized self-care list from chapter four to find something nurturing you can do in short periods of time.

Am I in pain?
- Follow up on medical or dental care through making an appointment with your health care provider.
- Take medication as prescribed or recommended.

Am I beating myself up for anything?
- Use the phrases from chapter two to remind yourself that we're always learning and mistakes are part of the growth process.
- Read the mission in chapter four, Speak to Yourself like Someone You Love, for a reminder of how to be more gentle on yourself.

Have I smiled today?
- ☺

100 Ways to Be Kind to Your Child

This comes from a hugely popular post on my *Bounceback Parenting* blog. So many people related to these simple ways to show love that I even created a poster of it, which you can still find on the blog (bouncebackparenting.com/100-ways-to-be-kind-to-your-child).

When I wrote this list, I was in one of those exhausting phases of parenting when days were going by in a blur and I often went to bed feeling defeated and guilty. Thus, these ways to be kind are not complex or fancy; they are basically a reminder to myself of the simple ways I can connect with and be there for my children. Many of them will remind you of ways you are already showing love to your kids.

100 Ways to Be Kind to Your Child

TELL YOUR CHILD:
1. I love you.
2. I love you no matter what.
3. I love you even when you are angry at me.
4. I love you even when I am angry with you.
5. I love you when you are far away. My love for you can reach you wherever you are.
6. If I could pick any four-year-old (five-year-old, six-year-old . . .) in the whole wide world, I'd pick you.
7. I love you to the moon and then around the stars and back again.
8. Thank you.
9. I enjoyed playing with you today.
10. My favorite part of the day was when I was with you and we _____.

SHARE:
11. The story of their birth or adoption.
12. About how you cuddled them when they were a baby.

13. The story of their name.

14. A story about yourself when you were their age.

15. The story of how their grandparents met.

16. What your favorite color is.

17. That sometimes you struggle too.

18. That when you're holding hands and you give three squeezes, it's a secret code that means "I love you."

19. What the plan is.

20. What you're doing right now.

PLAY:

21. Charades.

22. Hopscotch.

23. Board games.

24. Hide-and-seek.

25. Simon Says.

26. Twenty questions.

27. "I spy" on long car rides.

28. Catch.

PRETEND:

29. To catch their kiss and put it on your cheek.

30. That they have a giggle tank. Does it need filling?

31. That their high five is so powerful it nearly knocks you over.

32. That you are super ticklish.

33. That you are explorers in the amazing world of your own backyard.

34. That it's party day!

TRY:

35. To get enough sleep.
36. To drink enough water.
37. To eat decent food.
38. Dressing in a way that makes you feel confident and comfortable.
39. Calling a friend the next time you feel like you are about to lose it with the kids.
40. Giving a gentle touch to show approval.
41. Dancing in the kitchen.
42. To get your kids to bop to the music with you in the car.
43. Showing your kids that you can do a somersault or a handstand or a cartwheel.
44. Keeping the sigh to yourself.
45. Using a kind voice, even if you have to fake it.

READ:

46. A book of silly poems.
47. A story and then act out the plot.
48. Your favorite childhood book to them.
49. When the afternoon is starting to go astray.
50. Outside, under a tree.
51. With them in the library kids' corner.
52. The comic book they love that you're not so hot on.
53. About age-appropriate behavior so you can keep your expectations realistic.

LISTEN:

54. To your child in the car.

55. To silly songs together.

56. For that question that means your child really needs your input.

57. One second longer than you think you have patience for—or seventeen!

58. For the feelings behind your child's words.

ASK:

59. Why do you think that happens?

60. What do you think would happen if _____?

61. How shall we find out?

62. What are you thinking about?

63. What was your favorite part of the day?

64. What do you think this tastes like?

SHOW:

65. Your child how to do something instead of banning them from it.

66. How to whistle with a blade of grass.

67. How to shuffle cards—make a bridge if you can!

68. How to cut food.

69. How to fold laundry.

70. How to look up information when you don't know the answer.

71. Affection to your spouse.

72. That taking care of yourself is important.

Take Time:

73. To watch construction sites.
74. To look at the birds.
75. To let your child pour ingredients into the bowl.
76. To walk places together.
77. To dig in the dirt together.
78. To do a task at your child's pace.
79. To just sit with your child while he or she plays.

Trust:

80. That your child is capable.
81. That you are the right parent for your child.
82. That you are enough.
83. That you can do what is right for your family.

Delight:

84. Clean your child's room as a surprise.
85. Put chocolate chips in the pancakes.
86. Put a love note in their lunches.
87. Make their snacks into a smiley-face shape.
88. Make sound effects while you help them do something.
89. Sit on the floor with them to play.

Let Go:

90. Of the guilt.
91. Of how you thought it was going to be.
92. Of your need to be right.

GIVE:

93. A kind look.

94. A smile when your child walks into the room.

95. A kind touch back when your child touches you.

96. The chance to connect before you correct so that your child can actually hear your words.

97. Your child a chance to work out their frustrations before helping them.

98. A bath when the day feels long.

99. A hug.

100. You get to choose the next one! What is your favorite way to be kind to your child?

....

Ten Fantastic Conversation Starters for Your Family

One of the easiest ways to connect is through conversation. These conversation starters are great because they're entertaining and let you get to know one another while you're on a drive, waiting in line, or eating a meal together. Use one of these questions the next time you get a chance to chat with your kids:

What's something that our family is really good at?

What are you looking forward to about _____?

What was the [funniest, grossest, weirdest, happiest, saddest] thing you noticed today?

What would be the worst superpower to have? What would be the best superpower to have?

If you could be any character in a book, who would you choose? Why?

When during the day do you feel the best?

What season of the year do you like best?

Share a memory of one of your favorite birthdays (or other holiday).

If you could solve one problem in the world, what would it be?

If you could, what part of today would you repeat? What part of today would you change?

What do you think your [grandpa, grandma, or other faraway relative] is doing right now?

Online Headquarters

Find our online headquarters with bonus debriefing journal questions, printable reminders of the growth mindset, weekly check-in pages, and more at bouncebackparenting.com/HQ.

Acknowledgments

Thank you:

To all of the readers of *Bounceback Parenting*. Your stories, questions, and insights make me feel not alone. You are truly my inspiration every day.

To Lorien Van Ness—your wisdom is interwoven into every page of this book. Thank you for being everything from a sounding board to a coparent, and, most important, thank you for being my friend.

To my editor, Marian Lizzi—thank you for giving me this opportunity and for being so good at that editing.

To Mom and Mark, for filling me with the knowledge that I can do, build, make, and create. Your confidence in me gives me a foundation of strength.

To Georgia and Papa, for teaching me that you can never run out of love.

To Zoë and Scott—our sibling relationship is the kind I hope to encourage among my own kids. Thanks for being there for me.

To my colleagues online who've helped Bounceback Parenting become the platform that it is and who've always been generous in showing me the ropes and sharing your knowledge.

Thank you to Beryl Young, for friendship, guidance, and help with the grief and gratitude section; Dayna Abraham, for encouragement and inspiration; Doug Cunnington, for always listening; Sara O'Neill, for your knack of offering support at just the right time, and the members of my mastermind group, Jamie Reimer, Jill Riley, Trisha Hughes, and Courtney Slazinik.

To my kids, for all the ways you make me smile and for putting up with all that time Mama is working.

And finally, of course, to Michael. You are my person and I am better for being yours. Thank you for being my true love, my dashing husband, and my coadventurer.

Notes